Living in the Country Growing Weird

The Parks family, ca. 1962. Julie,

holding Greg; Dennis with Ben.

Photo by Richard Parks.

▲▲ University of Nevada Press

Reno & Las Vegas

Living in the Country Growing

Weird

A DEEP RURAL ADVENTURE

DENNIS PARKS

University of Nevada Press, Reno, Nevada 89557 USA

Copyright © 2001 by Dennis Parks

Photos © by Dennis Parks, unless otherwise noted

Manufactured in the United States of America

Design by Carrie House

Library of Congress·Cataloging- in-Publication Data

Parks, Dennis.

Living in the country growing weird : a deep rural

adventure / Dennis Parks.

p. cm.

ISBN 0-87417-484-8

1. Parks, Dennis. 2. Potters—Nevada—Tuscarora—

Biography. 3. Country life—Nevada—Tuscarora.

4. Tuscarora (Nev.)—Biography. 5. Tuscarora (Nev.)—

History. I. Title.

CT275.P382 A3 2001

979.3'16—dc21   2001001404

The paper used in this book meets the requirements

of American National Standard for Information

Sciences—Permanence of Paper for Printed Library

Materials, ANSI Z39.48-1984. Binding materials were

selected for strength and durability.

FIRST PRINTING

10 09 08 07 06 05 04 03 02 01

5 4 3 2 1

To Lois Ferry Parks (1906–1987), my mother,
and Aurora Tuscarora Parks (b. 2000), her great-granddaughter

Some nerve cells may die . . . changing a memory a little bit.
—PROFESSOR DAVID RUBIN, psychologist, Duke University

Contents

Illustrations

Acknowledgments

Special appreciation to my family, Julie, Ben, and Greg, who thankfully were quiet about any doubts and encouraged me with patience and love. And to friends who contributed so much through companionship, moral support, letters and visits, many of whom also volunteered their labors: Cliff Anderson (Nevada), Ron Arthaud (Nevada), Arturo Bassols (Delaware), Buddy Blatner (Pennsylvania), Bob and Karen Brown (Nevada), Lee Deffebach (Utah), Jay and Ruth D'Spain (California), Bud Eldridge (Nevada), Fred Elliott (Singapore), John and Goedele Fahnestock (Colorado), Bobby Gibbs (Nevada), Carl Hertel (New Mexico), Katy Hertel (California), Jerry Johnson (Nevada), Pete and Pat Kuentzel (Florida), Kurt LeMay (Nevada), Jan Heller Levi (New York City), James Linnehan (California), Michael Malter (Washington), Dee McBride (Nevada), Bob and Elise Misiorowski (California), Mack and Janalee Morgan (Florida), Sana Musasama (New York City), Margaret Norman (California), Denis and Tita O'Connor (California), Leonard Palmiter (Nevada), Audrey Parks (Florida), Pam Parks (Nevada), Valerie Parks (Nevada), Gail

Rappa (Nevada), Dennis Roberts (California), John Rovin (Texas), Jeff and Anne Schlanger (New York), Richard and Viviane Schupbach (California), Joe Soldate (California), Paul Soldner (Colorado), Gary Snyder (California), Myron Stahl (Nevada), Jane Suter (Florida), Sarah Sweetwater (Nevada), Greg Trousdale (Nevada), John Warfel (California), Larry Wisbeck (Nevada), John and Mary Will (Canada), Doug and Sharon Wilson (Illinois); and to those deceased: Gordon Bailey, Warren and Lisa Butters, Reggie Coffin, Nelson and Florence Foster, Roy and Inez Holaday, Archie Lani, Jim and Doris Murphy, Willis and Lois Packer, Earl and Della Phillips, Traw Roseberry, Louis Salat, David Schickele, Arnold Schraer, Charlie and Janie Stivers, Tom Suter, Nona Trembath, Lou Walker, Mark Wallace, Bud and Eunice Wilder; and to literary friends who read early drafts of the manuscript, offering suggestions and encouragement: William Fox (California), Franz Hansell (California), Anne Higgins (New York), and Kirk Robertson (Nevada).

Living in the Country Growing Weird

Tuscarora, looking north

toward Mount Blitzen.

The tall structure on the

slope behind the town is

the remains of a smelter.

Tailings from the mining

operation are visible to the

left of the smelter.

CHAPTER

Exiting the Freeway

Summer 1972: Julie sang softly, and I steered east toward Nevada. Our two young sons, Ben and Greg, fought each other in the backseat. The car surfaced above the L.A. Basin at the summit of Cajon Pass; we would sleep the night in our mountain home. Yesterday was a simile for our tomorrow: the simple preindustrial life. A potter and his family scratching their message in the dirt. I could visualize the mountains and the sagebrush clearly in black and white or sepia, no neon and no blood.

As I drove faster on through California's Mojave Desert, aiming for the town of Tuscarora in the Independence Valley of northeastern Nevada, I had no premonitions of the sex and violence that lay ahead. Yet, I was tense, a raw recruit anticipating small skirmishes with the elements before reaching armistice with nature.

A long drive. From time to time Julie knelt on the front seat and ministered to the needs of our boys in the back: adjudicating questions of ownership, wiping a bloody nose, distributing bribes. I did not know what she was thinking, though I trusted that she had a better grasp of detail than I did.

I was staring at the broken yellow line on asphalt ahead and glancing occasionally at the speedometer below. No accident or arrest should slow us down. My attention drifted to the animals I would soon be acquiring: rabbits, chickens, ducks, geese, pigs and goats . . . and a garden with a compost heap here, fruit trees there, berry bushes and all. I had no original thoughts or survival skills.

From 1968 through 1972 I had been employed as an assistant professor of art at Pitzer College, a progressive liberal arts college southeast of downtown Los Angeles. Full-time faculty members were required to teach three classes one semester and two the next. Most colleges classify such a light load as part time. Pitzer also had a generous sabbatical program: the first was automatic after four years; subsequent sabbaticals came every three years.

I was promised early tenure when I returned. Job security appealed to a middle-class core while challenging what was left of rebelliousness in a thirty-five-year-old latter born. Julie is also latter born, and we agreed that tenure looked like a life sentence.

Recalling the slogan "If you're not part of the solution, you're part of the problem" eased my conscience as we left the crowds, smog, and traffic jams. Southern California, the land of contrasts: Disneyland and the Watts Towers; brush fires in Malibu and fire bombs in Compton; ghosts of Aimee Semple McPherson and Charles Manson cohabitating. The population was diminished by four.

Julie had been employed as a nurse and was delighted to drop off all those white uniforms at Saint Vincent DePaul's as we packed for our move to the country. Ben and Greg were on the precipice of adolescence. A decade would slowly pass before those two would again be as malleable. We all agreed to the adventure. Of course I knew that after our rural fling, the old teaching job was there waiting for me.

Driving into Nevada from California reminded me of the summer of

1962 when we entered from the other direction, our VW bus loaded with all our possessions, including one boy in a playpen learning to sit up and the other on the front seat repeating a limited vocabulary . . . "See Lee, Gordon; roses are red, my love." Lee Deffebach, a painter we had known in Washington, D.C., wrote suggesting that on our way to California we check out an interesting ghost town she and her husband had moved to. "Only an hour off the highway."

We turned north off U.S. 40 at Elko and drove up into the mountains. After twenty-seven miles of emptiness, there was a junction with a sign, pointing left, TUSCARORA 25 miles. We climbed through another range of sagebrush-covered mountains until we dropped down into a canyon with a stream lined in willows and aspen. From here we entered a valley surrounded by mountain peaks. I almost missed the hand-painted sign pointing left, TUSCARORA 7 miles. These were slow miles maneuvering

Tuscarora, looking east from Hill '76 toward the Independence Mountains.

Tuscarora street signs. Photo by Larry and Joan Logan.

around potholes on a corduroy dirt road across the valley and halfway up a mountain.

I parked in front of the only building with a sign: TUSCARORA TAVERN—CLOSED. A local was in the street. He walked over, and I slid the window open and asked the first question that came to mind, "How many people are in Tuscarora?"

"Well, today . . . counting your family, it's thirty-five."

He introduced himself as Warren Butters, proprietor of the tavern, hunting and fishing guide, and owner of the electric company and telephone company. He also had units for rent. Julie asked directions to Lee's house, which wasn't hard for Warren to point out. There were very few structures. Since he was talkative, I followed him as he opened up the tavern, and I suggested that Julie and the boys try to find Lee.

Warren explained that we were sitting at the junction of Main and Weed Streets. If I looked east or south, I would be looking at the Independence Mountain Range. West and north lay the Tuscarora Mountains. To the north behind town I could hike to the summit of Mount Blitzen at 8,600 feet in approximately an hour and a half. The Tuscarora townsite was laid out on this particular spot by the mining interests that had employed workers in the miles of shafts directly below us. Between the 1870s and 1900, a silver boom drove the population to over 2,000; then a bust brought the tally down to two or three hundred. Toward the end, no one cared to count.

Tuscarora Tavern, the largest original structure still standing. Photo by Larry and Joan Logan.

I asked if he had been born here, "Nope. Drawn here in late '40s to do a little prospecting, then settled down." I excused myself so I could look around and get oriented.

No map of the town existed, but my survey calculated eight city blocks defined by an unpaved grid of Gold Street, Silver, West Avenue, California Street, Argenta, Clay, Weed, and Main. Mostly empty lots covered in desert weeds, rusty machinery, vintage automobiles minus wheels, and the occasional stack of bleached, splintered lumber. A few colorful travel trailers and mobile homes, less than a decade old, interjected that certain modernity that precluded Tuscarora's value as a setting for cowboy films.

Unoccupied stone house. Some of the original inhabitants of the town constructed their homes from local stone, an abundant and enduring building material. Photo by Al Higgins.

Shape rather than color was the memorable quality about the houses: small squares and rectangles with shotgun additions. A few with quaint false fronts, but mostly no-frills utilitarian. One or two had a veneer of flattened five-gallon metal cans shingling the walls and roof. After decades of little moisture the surface patina was reminiscent of contemporary skyscrapers in Cor-ten steel.

Architectural exceptions stood out. The tavern was a massive stone structure constructed from local rock. The hotel down the street had been moved twice from failed mine camps before reaching Tuscarora. This two-story building looked at home surrounded by a picket fence and towering Chinese elms and Lombardy poplars. On the far west end of Weed Street was a small elegant, high-ceilinged, red-brick home, best viewed from a block away. The front porch was only a skeleton, and the wooden addition out back had a collapsed roof. Uninhabited for half a century, yet emitting a whiff of potential. Definitely a fixer-upper town.

This town and the valley made me restive: the sunshine and the big sky, the quiet pace and potential. On the other hand, Julie saw Tuscarora as an attractive nuisance. She discovered abandoned mine shafts only a few baby steps off the road. These deep holes were, for the purpose of worrying, essentially bottomless.

I promised to be uncharacteristically overprotective. Then she agreed we could rent a cabin for a few weeks. My days were spent trekking in widening, concentric circles around the town, ostensibly prospecting for a clay deposit, but carrying a .22 caliber rifle in case I scared up a rabbit or a rattlesnake scared me. Mr. Butters assured us there were no poisonous snakes within a twenty-mile radius, but his physique didn't impress me as that of a man who hiked.

While I walked, Ben and Greg napped; Julie patrolled the streets, bent over, collecting rusty nails, jagged bits of metal, and sharp fragments of broken glass, which she tossed down the closest shaft.

Late summer 1962 we drove off, continuing a journey to California. Ben sang his new ditty, "Rice-A-Roni, the San Francisco treat," which

Unoccupied brick house. This structure has since been renovated and serves as the home of artists Ron Arthaud and Gail Rappa. The trees in front of the house died when the old town water system was abandoned in the 1960s. Photo by Al Higgins.

Headworks of an abandoned mine. The neighborhood of Tuscarora has many abandoned mine shafts, some of which have traditionally been used as dumps for trash. Photo by Al Higgins.

he'd picked up from the radio. I kept rural thoughts to myself. Why polarize a perfectly good marriage? There was no way we could afford to live in the middle of nowhere. I had found an outcrop of clay that might do just fine. Perhaps I could start a small school here. With time the boys would grow wiser and more responsible, develop outdoor interests, and mature into allies.

As I drove, Julie and I bantered lightheartedly about where we should settle on the coast. Mendocino was reportedly beautiful but rainy; San Francisco spectacular but expensive.

For a year and a half (1962–1963) we lived in the fog at Lover's Point in Pacific Grove by the Monterey Bay listening to sea lions bark and watching whales migrate north and south. I wasn't doing much so was surprised when a serious plan popped up. I should enroll in graduate school and become an art professor. Steady work, short hours, and long vacations.

Another year and a half passed quickly in Southern California while I completed the requirements for a Master of Fine Arts degree in Claremont. In 1965, I graduated into a seller's dream market. Academic jobs abounded. I accepted the offer from Knox College, Galesburg, Illinois, because facilities were in a new building where I had free hand designing studios, purchasing equipment, etc.—skills I didn't yet have but could be useful in the future.

After every move we made, Julie immediately accepted a job in a hospital or doctor's office. My income potential had always been more diffuse: part-time potter, substitute high school teacher or paper grader, art gallery sitter, orchid gardener, whatever. For the first time in six years of marriage, we both would be employed full time. I opened a savings account and hoped that Julie had no plans.

Neither of us considered Galesburg the finish line. The Midwest was flat and much too far away from Tuscarora. Vacations the previous three summers had mellowed Julie, and she didn't oppose my idea of trying to attract students to a school of pottery there. Perhaps her medical training recommended draining a boil rather that letting it fester.

The institute was named in utero: TUSCARORA RETREAT & SUMMER POTTERY SCHOOL. Wall posters were printed proclaiming, *A Chance To Escape & Explore!* A two-page Xeroxed brochure focused on answering basic questions: *Where is Tuscarora? What is Tuscarora? Why Tuscarora?* and *Who is Dennis Parks?* I was off and jogging.

Correspondence back and forth with Butters arranged room and board for students. Details, such as potter's wheels, kilns, glaze chemicals, would somehow have to be dealt with on site.

Propaganda was posted to art departments and art centers around the country encouraging aspiring potters to trust me enough and sign up for the month of July. (Through the years, enrollment ranged from a high of

Old privy covered with flattened metal cans. The dry climate of Tuscarora inhibits rust, and locals learned early to utilize and recycle available building materials.

Chimney of the old smelter on the slope of Mount Blitzen above Tuscarora. Mine waste and other locally found materials have become integral to Dennis Parks's pottery.

sixteen to a low of two. Inexplicably, the highs occurred when America elected Democratic presidents and the lows under Republican administrations.)

After returning to Knox College and teaching the 1966–1967 academic year, I resigned. An offer of an assistant professorship at Pitzer College tempted me back to California, closer to Tuscarora. We had made friends at Knox, and the farewell parties were gala. Late news came from Pitzer explaining that, unfortunately, funding for the position would be delayed for a year. Even this announcement, however, did not cancel the festivities. "No problem." I proposed another toast, "To gentleness." We planned to summer in Tuscarora; why not stay put, wait out the year?

Traditionally, houses in Tuscarora were named for the last owner who died there. For four summers we rented the Dora Lamar residence, home of a former postmistress and piano teacher. Included in rent was use of a weathered barn across the street. The bats were chased out, the dirt floor was shoveled clear, and the ground outside was leveled for kilns.

Owning a piece of property in Tuscarora had been a repressed desire: just a small place for four. Responses from locals, whenever I inquired, were not encouraging: "Nope . . ." or "Nothing now . . ." or "Don't know of a thing." Direct, but not hostile answers. I was an outsider and a potter, an unfamiliar profession that, quite reasonably, was not taken seriously, unlike cowboy, sheepherder, or bartender.

With time the social climate changed. Neighbors saw me up early, minding my own business, my pickup truck out by the old smelter where I gathered broken firebrick or a cluster of students around me in a dry streambed, shoveling red clay into gunnysacks. Once, Louie Salat came into the studio to watch pots being made and remarked, "So this is how you get so dirty."

Locals smiled and paused to watch Ben and Greg kicking rocks at each other as they ran up Weed Street. Locals cheered when the boys sicced their dog, Sophie, after terrified ground squirrels. Julie was hired

Photographed in 1962, Tuscarora's original "Glory Hole" lies just south of town. It was excavated by the Dexter Mining Company, which closed in 1903. In 1984, Horizon Gold Shares reactivated mining in this area, draining the Glory Hole for an open-pit mine that threatened to expand and consume the entire town of Tuscarora. After much controversy, this mining ceased in 1990, largely because of the falling price of gold, and the lake gradually refilled. Lake Lost Horizon, as locals call it, provides fishing and swimming for the community.

part time in the post office, and the town came to depend on her professional skills when minor medical emergencies arose.

One day Nona Trembath shouted to me from her front porch as I was walking by, "Boy, come over here." She used the diminutive for all males under Social Security age. "You interested in four-wheel drive? Go see Wilkins. He wants to sell his Rover. Moving to Carlin. New job."

Julie must have told someone at the post office that I was in the market for a reasonably priced, four-wheel-drive vehicle for transporting our sons to the one-room schoolhouse across the valley during the winter. Being a fan of British World War II desert films, I had admired the used Land Rover parked in front of Wilkins's home. I could envision myself at the wheel of just such a classic.

Jim Wilkins was taciturn when I asked him if rumor were true, but he nodded. I commented that I might be interested. Neither of us even hinted at enthusiasm. Jim suggested we go fishing tomorrow after he came home from work. It was his last week with the county grading a road from Tuscarora to the asphalt. He shook my hand, parting with, "You have the worms dug and be by my Rover at four."

I was right on time, which I worried might be a tactical error. Without speaking, he drove us five miles downhill to the center of the valley. This Land Rover was noisier than a pickup or a VW van.

After he parked, I followed his lead walking down to the water. This was my first fishing expedition on the south fork of the Owyhee, a tributary that seemed to snake and dogleg down the valley like a convoluted argument. Easterners invariably laugh when we drive over the bridge, and I point to the river, "There, there . . . see it?" They try to correct me with words like creek, crick, brook, or ditch.

The river can be forded in many spots with only one of your feet getting wet, but then at thirty- to fifty-foot intervals, the spring runoff has carved deep fishing holes. These depressions are the habitat of wily, pink-spotted eastern brook trout.

I wasn't terribly interested in catching fish that day. Without seeming eager, I wanted to question Jim about his asking price. Conversation was impractical. The fishing holes were too small for two men to stand shoulder to shoulder on the shore, and distances between the holes were too great for the nuances of bargaining.

My concentration became focused on hooking and landing fish, a mesmerizing activity. After an hour or so, out of the corner of my eye, I saw Jim walking slowly toward the Land Rover carrying his rod and a stringer of fish. When I caught up to his side, he tossed me the ignition key, "Give it a try."

The muffler would probably need replacing, but the steering felt tight, and the four-cylinder engine was responsive. If the price was right, this vehicle would be mine. I drove slowly up to his house and parked. When we finished unloading our catch and gear, Jim turned and spoke, "I also want to sell my house. I want to sell'm together."

"How much?" I asked tentatively.

"We go fishing tomorrow, and I'll let you know."

Again I accepted responsibility for digging worms, but on this second trip I was designated driver in both directions. As before, conversation was spare. I waited until the return leg to interrupt his silence with a noncommittal, "Have you come up with a price?"

He quoted a figure that seemed on the high side for a two-year-old vehicle but far too low to include any real estate. "Yep, that's what my wife and I agreed on. Hope it's all right. That'll give you the Rover, my house, and half acre it's sitting on."

I was quiet.

Jim spoke again, "And, you know the Plunkett place (he pointed with

Unoccupied wooden house. Many of the original buildings in Tuscarora have collapsed or their materials have been carried off for other use. Photo by Larry and Joan Logan.

The Plunkett house as it appeared when the Parkses arrived in Tuscarora. Dennis Parks's mother resided here for fourteen years.

his fishing rod three doors down Main Street). I've no use for't. I'll throw it in with the bargain." His cards on the table face up.

I answered that I'd have to talk this over with my wife. "It's a good deal," he said as I walked away. A grand understatement, I thought to myself.

Julie approved the deal before I had closed the front door, then paused and suggested sagely, "Perhaps you should make a counter offer 10 percent below Jim's asking price, so he'll respect you."

Her suggestion cost me another fishing trip. After I told Jim the price we'd pay, he needed to confer with his wife again. So, I dug more worms, and we returned the following day to the riverside for more silent comradery. He accepted Julie's price but with one caveat: "In cash."

A few years later the vacant hotel came on the market; the Bilbao family had moved off to a ranch south of Elko. Wife Bobby called asking if we would be interested in owning the building. Her asking price was so generous that I agreed immediately. Bargaining was no option. Respect in this rural community needed to flow from my other talents.

The Land Rover was a necessity, either that model or some other four-wheel drive. Only fourteen inches of precipitation is normal in a year, but most of it falls from December through March in the form of snow. Even though the county road leading in and out was bladed after each storm, its surface retained ice or slush or mud. Maps classify the road as "gravel," but this minor ingredient hangs in suspension, like lumps in brown gravy. My boys had to be driven to the one-room school on the other side of the valley. Julie needed to shop fifty miles away.

When ice fishing was on my itinerary, I navigated more distant roads that were never plowed and were classified as "dirt." On these expeditions I invited a neighbor, and we caravanned with two four-wheel drives, just in case.

Summer and fall the Land Rover was for frolic. Measurable rain seldom falls. Picnic climate. Perhaps for two weeks in August the thermometer rises into the mid-90s Fahrenheit; even then, at night we sleep under a light blanket. A major concern at this altitude is keeping warm. Cold is in the air for nine out of twelve months, particularly noticeable during those few weeks that drop below zero. Good for tulip bulbs, but hard on water pipes. Dogs are welcome in bed, because fleas can't live this high.

Travel books refer, geographically, to northeastern Nevada as part of the Great Basin, a unique area in the American West where all rivers and streams flow away from the ocean and inward to collect in lakes, swamps, or sinks. Most of Nevada is aquacentric, but not the Independence Valley. Our Owyhee River flows north into Idaho as a tributary of the Snake River, then flows west through Oregon and into Washington State, where it joins with the Columbia and finally spills into the Pacific Ocean. Before huge hydroelectric dams were constructed in the 1930s, spawn-

Unoccupied wooden house. The large trees were planted by the original occupants of the house. Photo by Larry and Joan Logan.

ing salmon made their way to the same holes Jim and I were fishing.

Hydrologically this valley is in the Columbia River drainage basin. Thus, Tuscarora should be considered a part of America's Great Northwest, but it doesn't look that way. We are high and dry with flora and fauna typical of a high desert. Nineteenth-century explorers compared this area with travel in Central Asia or Mesopotamia.

Water for the town of Tuscarora begins as snowmelt on the south slope of Mount Blitzen, flows underground, and resurfaces as artesian springs. Three of the largest had been channeled to flow into a lidded stock trough for storage. From there gravity forced the water through a four-inch underground pipe one mile into and through town, where it fanned out into one-inch pipes to connect with the houses. Households managed their own sewage with individual septic tanks, the overflow leaching underground into gravel-lined trenches.

I dwell on these details because I remember the poet Gary Snyder saying that the first step on becoming engaged with your environment is to learn where your water comes from and where it goes. In cities I never did. Just turn a faucet or press to flush. Contemplating origins and destinations can become a rural fixation.

Rural folks are closer to the workings of nature, partly to stay alive and partly from heightened curiosity. Nature is our entertainment. (I can't keep up with current films but never miss a sunrise.) Out here mankind is viewed as being separate from nature. If a range fire threatens to ravage the town or a mining company challenges our property rights, the citizenry coalesce; normally, however, everyone just waves from the front porch. Individuals who move into deep rural must be, *a priori*, a bit reclusive: those who stay long enough may grow outright misanthropic.

Certainly Julie and I were not questing a richer social life when we settled here. Not having a regular job was enticing: scheduling the pace of each day was appealing; living with fewer *shoulds* and *oughts* looked relaxing. Of course, large open space with few distractions is said to be the aphrodisiac of soul and imagination.

"Don't you get lonely? Don't you feel isolated?" are familiar questions.

"No," is the answer. In a strange, twisted way I feel more centrally located here than in urban America, like the axle of a bicycle wheel with spokes pointing outward. One hour of traffic-free driving puts me in Elko, a small town where there are enough stores for necessities and frivolity. For extravagance, the airport books one-hour flights to connecting hubs in both Reno and Salt Lake City. The world is open. Low-budget travel by automobile can put me in either of those cities or Boise, Idaho, in half a day. A full day behind the wheel, and we can be clinking glasses with friends in Denver, Los Angeles, or San Francisco. Usually just the sweet aroma of possibilities is sufficient.

In retrospect I can see that in my youth construction began on the intellectual foundations of a rural, reclusive life.

"I'd rather be blind than deaf," Coker said. "Not me," said the old man, "I likes to see the world. You can do without the talk." (*The Horse's Mouth*, 13)

Joyce Cary's novel was a gift on my seventeenth birthday from an eighty-year-old raconteur with an inscription encouraging me to explore. "Laurence Durrell did." Other books on my shelves are still dog-eared and marked up from when at nineteen I studied philosophy in Switzerland. I was a precocious underliner. Samples:

I have never lost an obstinate sense of detachment, of the need for solitude. (Albert Einstein, *The World As I See It*, 3)

Nothing of real value in the world is ever accomplished without enthusiasm and self-sacrifice. (Albert Schweitzer, *The Decay and Restoration of Civilization*, ix)

"I am convinced that to maintain one's self on the earth is not a hardship, but a pastime, if we live simply and wisely." (Henry Miller, *Big Sur and the Oranges of Hieronymus Bosch*, preface, quoting Henry David Thoreau)

"Arise, come, hasten, let us abandon the city to merchants, attorneys, brokers, usurers, tax-gatherers, scriveners, doctors, perfumers, butchers, cooks, bakers and tailors, alchemists, painters, mimes, dancers, lute-players, quacks, panderers, thieves, criminals, adulterers, parasites, foreigners, swindlers and jesters." (Helen and Scott Nearing, *Living the Good Life*, 2, quoting from Francesco Petrarch, *DeVita Solitaria*, 1356)

Such a bibliography gave me confidence that I possessed the underpinnings to thrive in the outback. Thoughts turned to the mundane. By

Unoccupied barn, overlooking Independence Valley to the east.

Two brick chimneys are all that remain of Tuscarora's "Nob Hill," where the town's wealthier residents once made their homes. The ravine in the foreground was the location of Tuscarora's Chinatown.

1972, our two houses gave a redundant sense of security for shelter and warmth; the Land Rover covered transportation.

For just one year, I would receive half salary and full medical coverage from Pitzer. A sufficient buffer. The summer pottery school expanded, adding a fall and spring semester; two students enrolled for both sessions. A Cecelia flew from Washington, D.C., and a Barbara drove up from Los Angeles. Also a friend, Joe, an art professor in Southern California, took a leave of absence to help construct a new studio and kiln. A front room in the hotel was renovated into gallery space displaying works for sale to tourists.

A vegetable garden would be planted; deer would be harvested. Fish were plentiful. Firewood would be chopped and hauled from the north slope of Mount Blitzen where an unusually large grove of aspen trees grow.

Tuscarora Tavern (rear view).

Parks's first pottery studio in Tuscarora was the carriage shop on the right, which was part of property he rented when he first moved to town.

Soon we owned a donkey, three Nubian goats, a gaggle of geese, a flock of chickens, and more. Ben and Greg joined the 4-H Club and after school drove the Land Rover down to the river to check their muskrat traps. Customarily children drove back roads as soon as little legs were long enough to touch pedals.

I wrote the dean at Pitzer requesting that a year of unpaid leave be tacked on when my sabbatical ran out. Months passed, and I wrote again to resign. We weren't returning anytime soon. Certainly when the boys reached college age, I would apply for another teaching job on some campus where faculty children were given free tuition. I watched my growing boys chasing goats or skinning and stretching their muskrat pelts. They were so young: I could procrastinate.

Still, as a father with a middle-class American upbringing, I worried. For example, how would I be accepted back at the academic table after having so abruptly picked up my chips and left the game? I would need to look very good on paper; I needed to appear current while I was out of it. This curriculum vitae must sparkle with ambition and achievement and, at the same time, downplay some insignificant years of unemployment. I spent time outlining articles that would be submitted to magazine editors, and I thought more and more about writing a book. "Publish or perish" would be covered. Also, I plotted a list of competitive exhibitions to which I would ship works: national and international venues. I trusted that compulsive behavior over time would build a cv thick enough to impress. I carried this ephemeral document like a passport, and as I do on foreign soil, from time to time, for peace of mind, I'd check to see where it was.

Tuscarora Hotel and Gallery. The main floor of the hotel provides gallery space for work by Dennis Parks; his son, potter Ben Parks; and Tuscarora painter Ron Arthaud. The hotel also offers lodging for summer pottery students and occasional visitors. This is the third location for this structure, which was built in Palisades, moved to Cornucopia, and finally moved again to Tuscarora in 1876. Before Parks bought it in 1971, the structure had served as a rooming house, brothel, hotel, and private residence.

In 1972 I needed a new studio. By moving into the Fern Bush residence, the more livable of our two houses, I lost use of the barn studio that went with the rental of the Dora Lamar place. Buckminster Fuller's domes were all the rage in the late '60s, promoted by Stewart Brand's *Whole Earth Catalog* and Lloyd Kahn's Shelter Publications, *Dome Book* 1 and 2. I decided to build on a level piece of land directly behind the hotel. The dome shape was appealing because: (1) the projected construction costs were low, (2) it appeared like an upside down bowl, possibly an inspiring space for potters, and (3) an enthusiastic response came when I proposed the dome idea to California friends. Six volunteers were selected and promised free room and board. Another half dozen drove into town uninvited but persuaded me to relent and allow them to pay room and

Parks's first Tuscarora studio (side view).

The Parkses' first home in Tuscarora. Poppies in the foreground are descended from flowers planted by the town's early Chinese residents.

board while they labored and learned. Though their help wasn't needed, the extra cash was.

The first new structure to be built in Tuscarora within living memory began with my driving a stake in the ground where I guessed the center of a geodesic dome should be. A thirteen-foot long string was attached, and the circumference was inscribed in dirt. Ten equidistant spots were measured and marked where foundation holes would be dug. A neighbor, Nelson Foster, stood watching. He was median age for locals, his late seventies, still active and curious. A prospector with little to show for years of chipping at rocks except, as it turned out, the skills needed to dig holes.

On groundbreaking day, the Elko County building inspector was in attendance. He read us the rules: each of the foundation holes must be at least three feet deep and one foot in diameter. My unpaid workforce grumbled about the depth. The inspector quoted regulations concerning structural integrity, earthquakes, and a freeze line. "I've never seen one of these funny buildings. I have to be careful," he said, glancing over his shoulder at a dozen long-hairs with beards.

"Call me before you pour the concrete. I need to measure the holes." He drove back to Elko.

Digging with pick and shovel into compacted rock and clay was drone work. Sparks flying from the steel pick and afterward precious little loose material for a shovel. Cursing replaced conversation. Nelson walked to center stage, kicked at a low pile of debris and said, "Why don't we dynamite? I gotta few sticks in the shed." The labor force applauded after throwing their tools aside.

Blasting was a new game. I envisioned Nelson planting a long red stick of dynamite where each of the ten holes was plotted. This would be followed by ignition, explosion, and—presto. But pyrotechnics by Nelson were labor intensive. I marveled as he took out his rusty pocketknife and neatly quartered a stick of dynamite, then with mallet and chisel created a hole barely large enough to insert a quarter stick of terror. He attached what he called "the blasting cap" with a foot or so of firecracker fuse. He lit first, then shouted, "Take cover!"

The audience sprinted behind sheds and privies, with Nelson bringing up the rear wheezing and coughing. (His lungs had been singed by German mustard gas in World War I near Épernay, France.) A dull concussion was followed by the patter-patter of pebbles on roof tops, like late August hail.

Everyone but Nelson was disillusioned when we advanced to inspect the hole. The ground was loosened in an almost perfect twelve-inch-diameter circle but to a pitifully shallow depth. Joe cleared rubble with two shovel scoops. Then Nelson dropped down to his knees, enthusiastically chiseling for a next shot.

Explosions punctuated Tuscarora's quiet for two days. Nelson's health appeared to improve with exercise. The unpaid laborers relaxed on a patch of grass under a distant apple tree with a cooler of refreshments.

Nelson accepted Joe as his assistant. Joe was a man close to the earth; his father had been a water-well driller and weekend prospector; before going to college, Joe had spoken proletarian as his mother tongue.

A tired Joe telephoned the county courthouse announcing that our foundation holes were prepared for inspection.

"Office is swamped with paperwork," answered the inspector. "I'm sure you boys did a good job. Just go ahead and pour your concrete."

I was delighted when Joe repeated the inspector's words and didn't understand why Joe's face flushed. Joe continued on, saying exactly what he told the inspector. These words were profane, unequivocal, and insistent. Basically he said that since we followed regulations to the letter, the holes would be measured by an inspector. Friend Joe quoted Joe Louis, "He can run, but he can't hide."

A county car arrived in Tuscarora after sunrise the following morning. When I walked down to the construction site, Joe appeared to be bobbing and weaving in front of the inspector; but coming closer, I realized he was innocently bantering and pantomiming the drama of chiseling, blasting, running, and digging. Joe was best in face-to-face diplomacy. I stood back.

The sun made dwarf shadows where we stood. To the east the inspector's car crossed the valley, a white dot trailing a rooster tail of yellow dust. Joe cracked a beer and filled me in.

"See here." Joe pointed to the blue permit card. "Walter initialed for the holes. Said he's awful busy and would appreciate if I'd look after the rest of initialing."

The studio was approved before it was built. Joe said, "I liked the guy."

My reply was close to that now attributed to Chairman Mao addressing Chairman Hua, "With you in charge, I'm at ease."

Construction proceeded without interruption.

Geodesic dome studio in the snow. The rear of the Tuscarora Hotel can be seen in the background (left).

But the dome wasn't big enough. I needed more studio space for my work. When students were around, they crowded me out, and there was far too much talk. Also their musical taste did not include Joe Cocker or Jimmy Buffet.

Soon I was drawing up plans for a modest, low, rectangular structure to be built with used redwood posts purchased from the Union Pacific Railroad in Elko and earthen blocks pressed from Tuscarora soil. The dome had fulfilled three-dimensional dreams of identifying with the landscape: from a distance the dome was just another small hill similar in shape to the familiar tailing piles left behind from nineteenth-century mining. The colors of the new studio would blend with the environment: weathered wood and earth.

A good reason for a right-angled building was that I missed corners.

Geodesic dome studio (interior view).

In a dome I was at a loss as to where to store nonessential valuables: those cardboard boxes filled with useless treasures such as broken blue bottles, shards of Chinese rice bowls, and fragments of cast-iron filigree. Some day I might need such detritus for sculpture. I wasn't ready to toss the past down a mine shaft. Corners would solve this dilemma.

A former Peace Corps volunteer spoke of an inexpensive hand-operated earthen block press that he and his companions used to create unfired bricks for homes in Belize. He had no idea where in North America I could buy one, so I wrote to Stewart Brand, editor of the *Whole Earth Catalog*. The item was not listed in his publication, but in the 1970s I could think of no one else to consult for such an unusual tool. A distributor was located in the Midwest, and I mailed a check for my Cinva-Ram earthen block press. Before it arrived, I needed to line up an energetic, unpaid work force.

Tuscarora Pottery School. Left to right: Dennis Parks's two-story studio, Tuscarora Hotel (rear elevation), geodesic dome studio, kilns.

Dennis Parks's studio (interior). Courtesy Shelter Publications.

Recruitment proved more difficult for construction of a simple rectangle than for the geometrically complex dome. Fred, a neighbor who was employed full time as a driller, said maybe he could help just a little on weekends. Michael, a summer resident from the Northwest who had worked long hours building the dome, replied perhaps, but he was planning a construction project of his own. Though Ben and Greg expressed youthful interest when the new block-making machine arrived, they were not enthusiastic. One of them remarked, "Dad, those plans look boring."

My second architectural drawing was more elaborate with perspective, cross-hatching, and watercolors. The redwood posts were represented by dark, vertical lines and the blocks drawn individually, then covered with a transparent, earth-colored wash. I added a second floor, of board and batten, redwood and cedar, which I painted as muted stripes of orange and brown. Windows, doors, an outside staircase, and a second-floor deck were detailed. Scaffolding would be rented.

None of the potential laborers had ever worked on a two-storey structure. Height proved irresistible. Fred showed up after work and began digging foundation holes; then Ben and Greg sifted this dirt to remove unwanted rocks before mixing in portland cement and water and pressing bricks. Michael strapped on his carpenter's belt and set up a table saw.

At the end of that summer, all posts were in the ground and rose up to support the upper floor—a flat roof for several seasons. Half of the ground floor was enclosed with block walls, my interim private studio until the second floor could be completed.

The labor pool was transient: neighbors moved, and the boys went off to college. I enlisted former students, visiting artists, relatives, anyone idle and enjoying the hospitality of The Hotel—two nieces en route to Reno; John, an itinerant potter/carpenter between paying jobs in California and Colorado; Richard, the professor of Russian; Mack-the-Hammer, husband of a student; Pete and Pat from Miami (he serenaded with the tuba during his breaks), and the temporarily unemployed in town such as Tommy-Toothbrush and his Sweet-Pea Jane and Joe-Joe-the-Dog-Faced-Boy, a bearded art student looking for work in the mining industry. I was nicknamed Big-and-Mean, presumably referring to my attempts to hurry the job along.

The crew was a fairly consistent mix of generalists. The few who knew carpentry would choose a helper and go right to work. The inexperienced majority were trained to mix and press the earthen blocks. By necessity, rules for unpaid labor were loose. A single regulation was enforced for safety and efficiency: no cold beer until a minimum of two hundred blocks was made. Normally the quota was filled by lunchtime.

The building took seven years to complete. Though the project was labor intensive, this was not what slowed construction. Earth for the blocks was free, but the flow of cash needed for cement, lumber, insulation, wiring, windows, and nails was intermittent and as unpredictable as the summer weather in the mountains: mostly sprinkles and very seldom a cloudburst.

With such help from friends a clearing was being made in the wilderness fifty-two miles off the freeway north of Interstate 80.

2

CHAPTER   Animals and Assassins

No man is free who has an animal. —HELEN AND SCOTT NEARING, *Living the Good Life*, 27

That quote is probably good, true advice, but I have grown happier in my rural life disregarding some warnings. We owned a quarter-acre next to the Fern Bush residence. The former owner had fenced a dozen cattle in one corner, raising them on baled hay. Instead of wheelbarrowing load after load of manure to a more convenient spot near the house, I moved my garden to the fertilizer. The remaining open space lay green with native grasses and flowering weeds. I saw where goats should profile grazing; ducks, geese, and turkeys ranging free nibbling on sprouts and scratching for seeds. I converted a shed where hay had been stored into a chicken coop with new high roosts and low nesting boxes.

What little knowledge I had of animal husbandry was gleaned from magazines such as *Goat Breeders' Digest, Mother Earth News, Countryside, Organic Gardening, Rabbit Journal,* and that genre. Ben and Greg counseled with pamphlets and catalogs pilfered from 4-H meetings. Through my living room window I visualized my lot alive with animals furry and feathered in bright and subtle hues. I imagined bleating, cackling, quacking, blending with peeps from truly wild birds. "Ee, eye, ee, eye, oh."

Ben and Greg never agreed on a single breed of chicken to order, so we varied: Giant White Orpingtons towering above the grass, Polish Cresteds strutting around like titled boyars, common Rhode Island Reds chasing flies and grasshoppers, and humble Aracunas with Latin American origins confident in their superiority by producing pale blue and yellow and green eggs.

Through the mail a minimum order of baby chicks arrived in a perforated cardboard box enclosing twenty-five little ones. The cheeriest time of year in the post office was when chicks arrived. At home there was always a letdown after I carried the boxes in and opened them to pluck two or three deceased and trampled babies from a corner.

The fluffy chicks grew less cute before they sprouted handsome mature plumage. Their adolescent personalities exhibited a dark side. Gangs of large pubescents would surround a smaller sibling, then take turns pecking at the head and eyes until the little one dropped belly up to the floor. Evisceration followed. This abhorrent behavior seemed less evil than demented. When hens finally matured, they mellowed; but macho roosters transferred aggression toward humans. Those were first on my chopping block.

Personally, I find a disagreeable anatomical feature in birds, who are created with a minimum of orifices: a single one for urinating, defecating, and producing farm-fresh eggs. All in all, a pet chicken is an oxymoron.

Fried, casseroled, or barbequed, Julie's chicken was richer in flavor and texture than store-bought alternatives, reason enough to cast a blind eye to barnyard mayhem. We are what we eat. So are chickens. Ours were sculpted from generous offerings of freshly ground corn and wheat mixed into a thick gruel with goat's milk. In season I tossed wild watercress over the fence for snacks.

Killing livestock should be unpleasant, and it is. I've asked Julie to disperse our animals and feed me vegetarian if ever I do not procrastinate when it comes time to slaughter. No variation in technique alters the conclusion. The executioner in Utah asks, "Would you prefer to be hung or shot?"

As a youngster I witnessed Grandmother Parks in Tennessee dispatching fowl by wringing necks, wings and feathers flying like pinwheels before her blood-spattered apron. Inez, an Iowa native, suggested I hold the chicken upside down, lower its head to the ground and step firmly, then pull with all my strength. A ranch hand wandered by one fateful morning and proposed an Idaho uncle's technique: insert ice pick between upper and lower beak, then push hard, driving the pick up into chicken's tiny little brain. "All them feathers just loosen up and fall out. No need to dunk 'em in scalding water." He declined to demonstrate.

Death in my chicken yard was not experimental, but rather a protocol: dependable, humane, quick, and simple. I donned my black leather coat, downed a single shot of bourbon, and lifted a chicken to where its neck rested momentarily on a log. Whack with the French meat cleaver. The head rolled to the ground by my feet while I tossed the headless torso yards away where uncoordinated it flopped, jumped, and cartwheeled, probably much like the Girondins, Robespierre, Danton, Louis XVI, and Marie Antoinette.

All other birds—ducks, geese, turkeys, and guinea fowl—were fed well and protected, as best we could, from marauding predators, such as raccoons and weasels; and when the end came, they, too, were dispatched with revolutionary dignity. "Chant de guerre pour l'armée du Rhin."

After death came Julie with a caldron of near-boiling water. She held the fowl by their legs and dipped deep to loosen feathers. She plucked as I chopped off another head. This division of farm labor was never challenged even during the divisive 1970s and '80s, when sexual wars raged in cities around us.

One cool summer evening, while we sat in the yard watching the sunset with a gathering of California guests and pottery students, someone threw out the suggestion that it seemed about time we ate one of those fat turkeys. The flock was mature, with one particularly tall tom whose head poked above the others.

Next morning Ben and Greg crept into the field, gobbling their best imitations, and captured the bird. After the gate was latched, the turkey was released onto the lush lawn for a final few hours of frolic.

Adult festivities began earlier than normal after I brought out a gallon of red wine and a tray of paper cups. The lid was unscrewed and a round poured. "Za mir" (to peace), shouted friend Richard, a professor of Russian at Stanford University. I had hoped a few glasses of early morning wine would encourage volunteerism for the plucking phase, since Julie was occupied with preparing side dishes.

This particular vintage proved unpopular. No one returned for refills. The taste was sweet, with that bouquet hinting of artificial preservatives. I noticed Richard turning his back and pouring wine into the flower garden, and soon others followed his initiative. I went back to the kitchen looking for bottles of cork wine, and when I returned a crowd was gathered by the flowers watching the turkey peck at a patch of dark, moist earth. A full cup was then placed next to the bird, who drank long and deep in turkey fashion: fill beak, raise neck, and down the hatch. Ben and Greg giggled and remarked on the penile symbolism in the turkey's neck action: skin texture was certainly suggestive.

Turkey proved too slow a drinker for this crowd. A cereal bowl full of croutons softening in cheap red wine was presented with a challenge, "Let's get'm drunk." Turkey could not resist and soon was into the spirit.

After he had pecked his bowl clean, I noticed his wings were drooping. His thirst sated, he hopped unsteadily into the shade of a Chinese elm, sat down, fluffed his feathers best he could, and fell asleep. Guests lost interest and refocused on their own drinking. The volume of our conversation turned high, but turkey slept on.

When he finally awoke and returned unsteadily to an empty bowl, I offered water as an alternative, which he gobbled up, then staggered over and lay down again under the tree. A consensus formed in the mob: turkey must be offed before a fierce hangover set in. He was limp and compliant as I carried him away from the revelers, out behind a shed to the chopping block.

At the dinner table, guests debated the significance of participating in a moment of culinary history: marination from the inside out. No one could remember a better-tasting bird. Some said they had never liked turkey: the carcass couldn't have been picked cleaner by buzzards.

Jane Zack and Wendy Benkowski were two long-term intermediate pottery students, both of Polish extraction, specialists in Central European cuisine. For several years, Polish Easters were celebrated inside the Tuscarora Tavern under the girls' supervision: pirogi, kielbasa, charzan, mizeria . . .

So I was amenable when they proposed cooking a traditional soup from the old country. Duck Blood Soup didn't sound appetizing, but I assumed the name was referential to color or texture: an innocent dish with a misleading title totally unrelated to any of the ingredients, like Welsh Rabbit (a cheese dish). Then they asked me for a live duck.

First, Wendy telephoned her grandmother in a Milwaukee suburb for the authentic family recipe. Wendy repeated Grandmother's words to Jane, who took notes: "Hold duck under your left arm with its head over a bowl. . . . Drip hot candle wax on the duck's forehead until you have a circle at least an inch in diameter. . . . When this cools, pry it loose, and the feathers will come out. . . . Under the bare skin lies a large artery. . . . With a sharp blade make an incision. . . . When blood gushes, collect it in the bowl. . . . Quickly add vinegar and stir. . . . Start repeating Hail Marys to prevent the mixture from coagulating. . . . Add spices . . . " etc.

I walked outside to watch the girls running in circles around a single very frightened duck. Jane picked him up and held tight while Wendy tied a babushka around its beak and over the eyes.

The blood did not gush but rather dribbled at heartbeat rate. Finally the duck puffed out its breast, lifted its shoulders, and expired in the crook of Jane's arm. Wendy stirred the bowl as she rushed into the kitchen, all the while muttering Hail Marys. Before following her, Jane turned and handed me the dead bird with a request to dig a hole and bury it. Instead, I plucked the carcass and stored it in our freezer for another time.

Preparation was memorable, but I cannot recall the taste. I do remember a thick soup, dark and rich: a small bowl, half full, was adequate. I thought vaguely of the density in T. S. Elliot's poetry.

Fowl sex never looked erotic: some down and feathers flew, then the couple separated, and without glancing back at the partner, they walked in opposite directions. Rabbit sex, on the other hand, was a voyeur's dream. Partners jockeyed for position, female dominant, then male dominant, back and forth, back and forth, until finally the buck scored. BAAM. He would fall on his side paralyzed in a seizure and scream loudly as though he'd been kicked rather than climaxed. Seasoned breeders recommend against leaving the pair together in the same cage because incidences have been recorded where the doe, in afterglow, turns the buck over and bites off his genitalia, one warning I heeded.

The learning curve was steepest during those first ten years as I was settling into the country, steadily acquiring livestock. The written word was my only guide to raising rabbits because there were no breeders in this valley. I picked up a box of furry white bunnies at the Elko Airport, shipped from a breeder in Oregon. New Zealand Whites: a buck and two does. By then I knew from reading that (1) the gestation period for a pregnant doe is thirty-two days, (2) an average litter totals six bunnies, (3) a doe should be rebred when the litter is only one month old, (4) the most economical time to harvest (factoring vegetable protein input into animal protein development) is at two months, (5) rabbits are thirty times more efficient in this conversion than beef cattle, (6) keep buck and does in separate cages (reasons stated earlier).

Rabbits can be pet-quality animals. My brother-in-law in North Carolina lets one hop free in his home. If they are handled regularly while young, they remain cuddly into adulthood. Without early affection from humans they grow up to be biters and scratchers like mine. Before Ben and Greg enrolled in high school and boarded in Elko, some individuals did receive affection and grew up deluded about human intentions.

New Zealand Whites were purchased because they grow fast and look like laboratory animals with no distinguishing features or coloration. I knew I would be responsible for the harvest; I was hoping for no more individualization than I'd encounter in picking a row of cabbages.

Authors were unanimous in agreeing on a technique for harvesting rabbits: (1) hold the animal upside down, grasping the rear legs in your right hand; (2) firmly grasp the neck at the base of the ears with your left hand; (3) quickly push down with your left hand while pulling up with your right; (4) finally, cut the jugular vein to bleed out the carcass.

I visualized emergencies: what to do next if rabbit remained alive but a blinking quadriplegic. Pull again? Shoot or club the bunny? I needed a quick and sure technique. Guns make so much noise, and there is that rankness lingering in the air from the powder, sulphur, and saltpeter.

I hacksawed a short length of galvanized water pipe. With my left hand I firmly grasped ears with rabbit facing the horizon. I lifted him/ her high enough so back legs were pawing air; then with the pipe in my right hand I swung hard, aiming at the neck. The force of the blow pulled ears out of my hand, and rabbit flew through the air executing a 360° before flopping to the ground; out cold, eyes glazed, twitching slightly, like a sleeping dog having a nightmare. An incision was made swiftly under the jawbone, and blood pumped out involuntarily. Rabbit expired, and the worst was over. Skinning and gutting was a painless routine for both of us.

Perhaps being a Capricorn made my acquisition of goats inevitable: goats, knees, water, and other astrological arcana. Carl, an interpreter of the I Ching in California, thought I needed Maude and William. He presented them, and they became our breeding stock. The goats arrived on a

The Parkses' experiments in self-sufficiency included raising ducks and goats.

cold spring day. North wind blew a scattering of snow across frozen ground, and Julie lined a cardboard box with straw, which was placed beside our wood stove. Kids are as cute and warm as little children remembered. We didn't punish our goats when they trimmed houseplants or left pellets and puddles on the linoleum. We were experienced parents.

Within two weeks the weather improved, and the goats were moved into a tiny shed stacked high with hay for burrowing into at night. These

Nubians grew rapidly. William's coat turned black with white patches, and Maude's a glossy dappled brown. It wasn't often, but when they stood still and erect in the field, from a distance they resembled Picasso bronzes.

At their maturity I envisioned companions as faithful as dogs but more utilitarian. I built a milking stanchion for Maude and Julie, then purchased a colorful enamel bucket and a standard cheese press. Willis and Lois, neighborly cattle ranchers down the valley, fell into the habit of delivering a free stack of hay every fall, even though they didn't understand our choice of goats instead of cows or sheep.

From Carl I understood that goats lived for eight to ten years and could at any time develop antisocial behavior if they perceived that humans were ignoring them. I became intent on bonding early. Immature animals and children generally like me, without reservations.

The goats' field was sprinkled nightly with water, nurturing grass through the summer drought; hay was also thrown over the fence, and kids would nuzzle the back of my hand as I poured on rolled oats for garnish. During the day someone in our family could be seen scratching behind goat ears or giving a gentle back rub.

One summer morning as I began my daily jog, passing the goat pasture I could see Maude and William with their front legs up on the fence, and I heard their bleating. Perhaps we would all be entertained running together. I opened the gate and continued my run with goats following on each side as though expertly trained. Only occasionally would they stop to nibble on a branch of rabbit brush, a thistle, or a cluster of serviceberry leaves; and as we forded a seasonal stream they knelt to take a drink. They would sprint to catch up.

We jogged north past a derelict, rusty-grey, four-door sedan riddled with assorted bullet holes, referred to as "Bonnie and Clyde's," a popular backdrop for urbanite Polaroids. Maude bounded up onto the hood to strike a pose. I slowly jogged on uphill until the kids caught up. Maude and William seemed to already know their names when I called.

At the crest of Nob Hill I stopped to catch a breath. This ridge is barren of structures unless two brick chimneys and half a dozen crumbling stone foundations are tallied. In the nineteenth century wealthy mine owners and merchants chose this site to build their homes. Downhill, just on the edge of town, is a broad arroyo where the Chinese lived. Pottery shards and an occasional coin are all that's left.

While I mused, Maude and William were denuding a thick stand of chokecherry bushes. That morning is remembered clearly because it was the only outing the goats and I took when they obeyed my commands. I tried to repeat, but they ignored my entreaties, warnings, and demands. They had quickly learned the lay of the land and were enticed by side roads or they would disappear until I returned home to find our rose bushes gone and the low branches on a pine tree roughly pruned.

Goat sex must have taken place in privacy after dark; the pregnancy began to show. Also, an odor drifted downwind from William; his scent had changed in recent months from fresh outdoorsy pet to glandular billy goat. Maude was alienated, butting him in the head or ribs if he approached. The union had been consummated, and William became an ex.

Julie anticipated fresh milk for human consumption and worried about William's odor drifting into the milking shed. I negotiated with a neighbor for use of a small fenced bachelor pasture downwind from town where William would be comfortable.

Julie researched this subject of milk goats. Poodle shears were recommended for removing goat hair on and around the udder because hair transfers flavor. She also read (what I had told her all along) that does produce more when milked exclusively by women.

Twins arrived: one of each sex. Maude dutifully licked newborns clean and dry, then ate the afterbirth just as books said she should. Unexpectedly she refused to stand still for the twins to nurse. Maude abandoned her manger and returned to work grazing in the pasture. The responsibilities of super au pair were accepted by Julie. She milked out mother, then filled baby bottles and, six times each day, fed the kids.

Rancher Willis rode horseback into Tuscarora on his way north looking for strays, and I waved him over to inspect our new goats.

"Whatcha' goin' to do with 'em?"

"Plan to keep the doe and sell the buck."

"Basques roast 'em on a spit. Good as beef, only stringier."

A potential barbeque was not what I saw gamboling before me. Healthful milk and cheese were our goals, but I looked up recipes before making a final decision.

KID EN CASSEROLE
Take a little haunch and hang till tender. Cover well with flour, then put into a big iron pot, with as many vegetables of different kinds as you can get, 4 oz. butter, pepper, salt, and a glass of white wine. Cook very slowly and very thoroughly. Cook at the same time in an earthenware dish plenty of potatoes cut in pieces, sautéed in butter and well seasoned. Serve the kid in a large dish deep enough to hold most of the gravy, and the vegetables together with it or separately. (Andre L. Simon, *A Concise Encyclopedia of Gastronomy*, 444)

I telephoned Willis, and he returned to demonstrate how bucks are castrated and emerging horn buds removed from both sexes. He explained to young Greg how, if young goat testicles have been removed, goats grow larger and, later, the meat tastes better. Because goats play rough with each other, with no horns, there will be less chance of an accident. Willis spurred his horse and rode off. Greg made a pronouncement: when he grew up he would be either a cowboy or a veterinarian.

Next spring more kids were born. Greg assumed responsibility for docking and dehorning; Ben helped with feeding and trimming hooves; Julie milked twice a day, seven days a week; and when the young bucks reached six months old I was expected to dispatch them. I procrastinated, but at nine months kids approach adult size with muscle fiber toughening. Ben and Greg would sharpen knives while I walked outside clad in black leather coat, trailing a rope lead.

Out of sight from the herd I would drop a fistful of grain to tempt the kid to stretch his neck out and down, then I struck with a baseball bat. While he was unconscious, I knelt down, cut his jugular, and bled the carcass. Ben and Greg came with the knives and began the familiar task of skinning and gutting. There was no talk; these boys knew what they were doing from their experience in the fur trade with muskrats and mink. The quicker the skin comes off, the sooner a creature loses cuddly references. Liver, heart, and kidneys were saved; lungs were thrown to the dogs. The pelts were salted, rolled, and mailed to Salt Lake City for tanning. Later, this leather was tacked down to upholster the seats of potter's wheels.

Carcasses were hosed clean, towel dried, and laid out on a picnic table, where Julie took over as butcher, cutting and wrapping meal-sized portions in white freezer paper labeled roast, chops, stew meat, etc.

After killing I washed my hands of blood and hair; I might pull up a chair to the kitchen table, mix a drink, and mull over my carnivore side. Vegetarianism didn't make sense in country with only a three-month growing season. Contracting with others to slaughter begged the question. An omnivore's dilemma.

An editorial in the *Pit Bull Journal* took a position: "Don't breed if you can't cull." Raising dogs, however, is different; goats must be bred yearly in order to stimulate renewal of milk.

Julie was extracting two to three quarts per day from one goat, when for no good reason I bought her another mature doe who proved equally productive. Refrigerator shelves filled rapidly with quart Mason jars, all opaque white. Goats' milk is thicker and richer because it is naturally homogenized; but a subtle aftertaste of wild remains stuck to your palate.

After first taste I told Julie, "I like it, okay."

Ben and Greg said in unison, "Tastes like Maude's breath."

Julie went back to the book. First, she tried filtering the milk through fine-mesh cheesecloth, then she added the step of flash chilling in the freezer before storing the milk jars in the refrigerator. I commented that I thought the taste improved, and regularly poured a splash on morning granola; Ben and Greg would drink milk only out of store-bought containers; Julie went lactose free. To help my sons overcome a food prejudice, I surreptitiously mixed goat and cow together in a standard milk carton. Both boys gave up drinking milk.

Cheese making required large quantities of goat milk, which we had; but, unfortunately, after curdling, pressing, waxing, wrapping, and aging for sixty days, the cheese was rank. Consensus had me put on the leather killing coat, bag the cheeses, and find a deep mine shaft.

Following these failures, goat milk was carried to the chicken house, where I was greeted with enthusiasm. One pint a day was saved in the hotel refrigerator for a student whom Maude was curing of a stomach ulcer.

My family developed a taste for the sublime goat meat. Barriers of gender discrimination fell the morning I slaughtered my first doe kid. Goat husbandry took on new purpose. When the student was cured and left Tuscarora, Julie stopped shearing the underside of milk goats and used the gadget exclusively for family haircuts.

In rural culture there is expectation that firstborn sons, at a specified age, step forward into an adult role. At age fourteen Ben looked ready (quiet, self-reliant, and tall), and the day came when I needed an extra set of strong arms to assist in slaughtering a very difficult goat. Somehow we had neglected to dehorn this animal. When goat horns grow long, any attempt to saw them is not only painful for the goat but unsuccessful because the horns will grow back.

This goat's horns rose high from the forehead, then narrowed, arching back to points just above his shoulder blades. These horns protected his neck from a baseball bat more effectively than the face mask on an umpire.

The biblical option: lead your goat to a mountain top and carry a long, sharp knife. Ben walked ahead into our pasture, mumbling to himself and calling goats by name. Nannies rushed forward with kids following, jumping, bumping, and tripping behind. I spoke, "Put your rope on that one. You know, the black one with the horns."

"Clarence?"

"Yeah, that one."

Ben and goat alternated leading and following while they maneuvered through a gate and out to the road on the far side of the milking shed. I knelt by the goat's flank and reached under his belly to grasp the opposing legs. With a sudden lateral pull and a short scuffle, goat was down, with me straddling his rib cage. The kid lay still, shocked by my uncharacteristic playfulness. Ben opened his Boy Scout knife.

I rubbed my finger under the hinge of goat's jaw. "Right here under this bump. Quickly, and the goat'll hardly notice." Knife plunged: goat screamed. I was knocked on my back looking up at a goat in the air. Ben stood to the side, wiping a bloody blade on his trouser leg.

When the goat landed on all fours, he began rotating backward in tight circles, uttering unfamiliar, bestial curses. I tackled and restrained him, my right hand grasping horn and left clasping his mouth shut. I was rocked from side to side as the wounded and dying creature made a final, pitiful attempt to stand. My fourteen year old stood over me and shook his head.

I worried. Could I be a father who was, so to speak, bonsaiing his children, trimming urban roots, and then twisting the emerging branches? Ben and I never spoke about this goat until he had graduated from college. We were sitting in our Tuscarora backyard looking up at an empty pasture while he listed courses he had taken at Stanford: Nietzsche, Marx, Sexual Mores, Money and Banking. "You can quarry a bit from all experience." A pause before he changed the subject. "You and Mom really out of the goat business for good? They sure were fun animals to have around."

"Do you recall helping me slaughter the goat-with-horns?" I asked. He looked blank and confused. I jogged his memory with a sprinkling of particularly loathsome details.

"Oh, yeah, yeah. I believe I do remember that." Conversation turned to undergraduate reminiscing about animals on Stanford's campus: horses for the horsey set; a barnyard of cows; squirrels in the trees; and sometimes coastal deer on the golf course. He told me how his roommate liked to shout and point, "Hey, Benner, look there . . . wild animals . . . KILL, KILL."

"I'd grunt and roll my eyes so everybody could have a good laugh. You know, Dad, all those guys grew up around cities. They knew absolutely nothing about animals. I used to love to put them on about how much frontier knowledge I had; how good a man I was with a gun and a knife; how I could be dropped any place in the mountains and I knew what to do to live off the land. It wasn't all true, but these urban types ate it up." Father stopped worrying.

Ben was right about the possibility of living off this land. Certainly there is evidence that migrating bands of Native Americans did so for centuries. In this valley alone there is a variety of meat dishes to choose from: mule deer, antelope, hare, rabbit, pica, marmot, raccoon, porcupine, and ground squirrel. Julie has cooked up samples from time to time. But these native herbivores are eaten primarily by local mountain lions, bobcats, and coyotes, with leftovers scavenged by eagles, buzzards, ravens, and magpies.

One day Nona caught me driving out of town with a rifle in my gun rack, and she waved to stop me. As far as she was concerned I could shoot any animal I wanted. "Except a porcupine. You wanta save'm for emergency. They're slow . . . 'bout the only creature a hungry prospector can corner and beat to death with a stick." Lore to remember.

Porcupine is reported to be delicious cooked in a campfire. First the animal is packed in a thick shell of moist clay with small holes poked in each end. Three to four hours on a bed of medium-hot coals and turned occasionally. Exact duration determined by when no more steam is emitted from the holes in the clay. The quills stay imbedded in the shell when the clay is broken open. Garnish with watercress from a nearby stream. This same procedure can be followed with ground squirrel; of course cooking time will be shorter. Purists delay eviscerating either animal until after cooking.

Nature offers many warm-blooded edibles, but on Julie's menu only mule deer has been a staple. Over the years we developed a close, symbiotic relationship with the local herd. In early September after frost has nipped photosynthesis out of sensitive crops like squash and lettuce, the only harvestable plants left are brussels sprouts and cabbage. Under cover of darkness, deer wander down out of the hills and slip into town, browsing on fallen crab apples and pears, but before returning, they balance their diet with mouthfuls of brussels sprout tops (my favorite, too) and nibbles from the crowns of cabbage. Footprints of an extended family remain in the garden. Hunting season opens in early October.

When I decided tit for tat, the only firearm I owned was a .22 caliber rifle, which I regularly brandished to frighten rabbits from the garden. More firepower was needed for deer, so I borrowed a friend's 30-30 lever action, and he instructed me on use and safety. Discharging firearms within three hundred yards of buildings is against the law, so I walked next door for directions from the old-time hunting guide, Mr. Butters. His wife, Lisa, said he was out, but she pointed north toward Mount Blitzen. "You drive up Nob Hill, follow the road east along the mountains, then in half a mile or so you'll see little roads leading back into canyons."

She may have been more specific, but I remembered only general directions. All canyons look alike to newcomers.

Ben and Greg were allowed to sit on the front fenders of the Rover, scouting for deer. I drove slowly out of Tuscarora. When we reached the first canyon, I stopped on the far side of a trickling stream and picked a shopping bag full of watercress. We continued up a rutted road until it

Julie and Dennis Parks, ca. 1969. Photo by Larry and Joan Logan.

dead-ended in a grove of aspen. No deer sighted. I parked. The boys jumped down, ready to hike, but had to wait while I loaded the maximum six shells into the rifle.

As we made our way through sagebrush, large boulders, and loose gravel, I repeatedly shouted at the boys to come back and stay close so they wouldn't be in the line of fire when we saw a deer. I had not hunted as a youngster with my father, so I was making up rules as we climbed.

At the crest of a hill I declared a rest. I scoped down into a shallow crotch of a canyon thick with tall sage. Nothing. Greg disagreed. He thought he saw movement. "There!!! Right there . . . " A single deer stood up, turned and looked back. No horns. Nevada law allowed harvesting either sex, but bragging rights in the tavern came with antlers— tall and wide and with lots of points.

Ben and Greg stopped talking when I clicked off the safety and aimed. The doe was very close . . . like shooting at an opponent in a tennis match who is headed rapidly up into the stands. I missed, and deer disappeared over the next ridge, along with four of the six bullets.

Another deer, awakened by this noise, started for the same exit. One of my boys shouted, "Look, Dad, HORNS." I shot and missed; I couldn't see where or how far off target. My final shot was dead center and high, but so was the deer, at the apogee of a bounce. The buck hung still in midair, rotated till his legs pointed skyward, then suddenly dropped out of sight in the sagebrush.

Ben and Greg ran like bird dogs and, when they located the remains, shouted back, "He's not moving, but come look at his eyes. They're wide open." No death throes: no sounds. A small bloody hole in the back of his neck. Ben grabbed the left antler and I the right, and we started dragging the carcass downhill toward the road. When we reached the Rover I conceded that our first deer ought to be draped over the hood, even though I had heard that the engine heat did it no good. This was only a short drive.

Butters was standing on his front porch when I parked across the street by our back door. He walked over, looked at the deer, counted points on the antlers, ran his hand down the flank, and asked, "Don't you know enough to field dress him?"

"Excuse me?" I replied. Butters explained how everyone knows that the intestines should be removed immediately after a kill; also the scent glands on bucks' ankles should be cut off.

"Meat'll taste better."

I thanked him and changed the subject to my appreciation for his wife's directions. "Where'd you go?" he asked quizzically. I elaborated.

"Why, that's the least likeliest place in this country to look for deer. Lisa never told you to go there. The next canyon to the east is where she meant. That one's full of deer."

Both Warren and Lisa have since passed away, but that small watershed where I was misdirected is still referred to around town as Least Likely Canyon. He was correct; deer are not usually there.

With experience I also learned that the clean final shot I fired that day was a singular event. Dumb luck. Subsequent Octobers are remembered for the carnage: deer mortally injured but still moving; deer limping, falling, rising, and falling again; legs blown off; intestines trailing; and always, when I caught up, the deer was still breathing and blinking.

Carnage from those years of hunting flashed back both times a gun was pointed at me. After each incident I could imagine the mess I would have made. With the first potential assassin I tried to save my skin by calmly listening to him berate me. Still he pulled the trigger (missed). The second, I cursed, turned, and walked away, trusting that in the West no one shoots a man in the back. I have not formulated a strategy for the future.

All experience is great providing you live through it. —ALICE NEEL, *painter*

Charlie, the second gunman, was a retired jailer who moved into a vacant house in Tuscarora two days after the owners, Nelson, the dynamiter, and his wife, Florence, were killed in a freak freeway accident.

Charlie claimed to have proof in writing that the building was his. No heirs appeared quickly to dispute him. Once he settled in, his days were divided almost equally between sitting home in front of TV and patrolling our streets armed with a back-pocket pistol.

For the first few years neighbors viewed him as just another eccentric, no threat to rural tranquillity. I always waved and spoke when his patrol passed our property, though he seldom reciprocated. "Old eyes and ears," was Julie's assessment.

Charlie's only buddy was a transient named Smitty who rented a small one-room stone house similar in size to Theodore Kaczynski's notorious hideout. Often Charlie paused and chatted while Smitty continued working on the transmission of his mid-1960s Cadillac. Reportedly Smitty never stayed in one town very long. He was what the English refer to as a "remittance man." His mother in Boston sent living money as long as he lived far away. From appearances, he ate well. His only complaints were about a bad back.

To facilitate such a large man with a disability working on the underside of an automobile, he jacked the Cadillac up and over until it rested on the passenger side. Then he could proceed, sitting comfortably in a straight-backed chair. Of course, when the car was back on its wheels, the crushed doors wouldn't open; but he brushed this off by explaining that he never picked up riders anyway.

Smitty owned a mongrel dog, named Brownie, who often followed Charlie when he left to continue his familiar pattern through the streets of Tuscarora.

One lazy Sunday morning I was firing a kiln. Every hour I'd walk down Main Street to my studio to check on the rise or fall in temperature. Our dogs, Mother Mean and her pup, Iris, begged to accompany me. Returning up the street, dogs were trotting a few yards ahead when suddenly Smitty's dog appeared out of the underbrush, dashing directly at Iris full speed with tail high and jaws open. Iris rolled on her back, pinned down by Brownie's teeth. Without hesitation Mother Mean entered the fray by latching onto a brown ear and then lying down. Brownie was quickly neutralized, and Iris was free to stand and shake off dust before retaliating with gusto and impunity. She concentrated on the perpetrator's tender underbelly.

I refereed by shouting at all three, "Stop it! Right now! Stop it!" They ignored. Meaner lay still as a sphinx locked onto Brownie's ear while he kicked all fours in vain attempts to ward off Iris. I commanded my dogs to "Come!" I jumped up and down while repeating the commands. I kicked both of them. Iris retreated to the other side of the road, only to begin barking at the fray. Meaner remained attached.

(Later I was told how to separate dogs by sprinkling ground black pepper on their noses. Then I knew only enough to keep my bare hands away from their muzzles.) I grasped Meaner's rear ankles and lifted high, hoping she would release. Brownie, attached and half suspended, shrieked. My back hurt. Onlookers gathered. Charlie walked slowly from the west with his hands behind his back while from the east Smitty came huffing up Weed Street with a spanner wrench swinging at his side.

As Charlie stepped closer, his right hand rose, gripping a small black pistol pointed directly at me. I yelled, "Put that damn thing away and help me."

Calmly he replied, "I'm goin' to shoot you and your miserable dogs."

"Don't act like a crazy old fool. Put that fucking thing away and help me."

Smitty was bent over behind Charlie, catching a breath; then he raised his wrench hand, and Iris backed further up the street. Charlie clicked off the safety on his pistol.

"You're fucking insane," I said just before Meaner opened her mouth and Brownie flopped to the road. Charlie glanced down to where Smitty was examining his companion's ear. I hastily tossed Meaner in the direction of home. I followed slowly behind, cursing my dogs. A long half block and I reached my mother's house. She had moved here from Southern California a few years earlier, and we gave her the smaller of our houses, the Plunkett Place. Mother was standing amid flowers in her greenhouse. My closest refuge.

Dogs at my heels I stepped in and closed the front door. "Did you see what was going on out there?"

"You men should all have your dogs on leashes."

"I mean Charlie and his gun."

"I watched it all. He wasn't going to shoot you."

"He said he was."

"You always did exaggerate."

Such confrontations can only appear melodramatic when the barrel is pointed at someone else.

Soon thereafter Smitty completed repairs on the Cadillac's transmission, and with Brownie still bandaged they drove off to Southern California and were never heard from again.

I purchased a highly regarded text, *The Koehler Method of Dog Training*, and Charlie ceased patrolling the streets of Tuscarora.

There was even more drama the first time a gun was pointed at me. Tammy Wynette sang "Stand by Your Man" in the background. The song is not a musical equivalent of Tchaikovsky's *1812 Overture*, but the weapon aimed was not firing blanks.

Midnight in June: bright and cloudless. Nevada must have at least twice California's allotment of stars. I was lying in bed listening to Nature: outside the soft rhythmic burping of bullfrogs in the flower bed, and in the ceiling above the scratching and scampering of pack rats tidying up. Normal sounds, which may gently awaken me and then slowly lull me back to sleep.

I had been prone for hours, and only gradually did I become conscious of a lyrical human voice coming through the wall.

She sang of love and forgiveness.

I fluffed the pillow and buried my head.

She continued on about advantages of sleeping with a partner on cold nights.

Jukebox philosophy played too loud on a warm summer night.

Tammy complains about the plight of being a woman.

Julie was next to me, feigning sleep. A pause, and then Tammy started repeating herself.

I heard giggles coming from the boys' bedroom. Julie's eyes were
closed, but her toes wiggled, and she asked, "Who's playing that music?"

"How should I know?" I got up and felt my way across the room to a
window.

A pickup truck was parked in front of Butters's house with its hood
up and a bare light bulb suspended above the engine. A body was draped
over one fender with cowboy boots dangling.

"Must be Butters's handyman."

"Hippy-Hating-Harold?"

"Who else?"

"Could you go over and ask him to turn the volume down?"

Just then the music stopped, and I watched Harold slide off the
fender, walk behind the truck to his car, and open the driver's door. He
sat down but left the door ajar.

"I don't know what he's doing now."

I walked over to the door of the boys' bedroom, knocked loudly, and
asked if they wanted me to help them calm down. "No, no."

Back to bed. I slipped under the sheet and lay there thinking about
the work I needed to complete in the studio and how badly I wanted a
solid sleep.

Tammy complains again about a woman's lot.

Harold had rewound the tape.

"Can't you reason with him?"

More female logic. How would I convince a man who is belligerent
by day to be obliging in the middle of the night?

Harold was a stranger who had wandered into the tavern the previous
fall. His first day was spent sitting on a stool in front of the bar, and the

next day he was standing behind it polishing glasses. It was not unusual for Butters to hire a homeless person during hunting season, but Harold stayed on. No one asked where he was from or where he was going. I noticed several of his fingers were missing digits, evidence that at one time he had probably been a woodworker. He drank only Budweiser. When he spoke, it was always the same, "What do you want?" He slept in the extra bedroom of Butters's home, space available after Butters's wife had left him.

Harold and I differed: he was a head shorter with mid-length gray hair, greased and combed straight back; what little hair I had was shaved clean; my full beard and mustache contrasted with his smooth face. He seemed more disagreeable around persons who were taller, younger, more conversational, less hirsute or more hirsute than he. Long-haired students gave Harold that alliterative title, Hippy-Hating. Harold was probably also anti-Semitic and racist, but Tuscarora didn't have those demographics.

I lay in bed listening to Tammy Wynette and pondering diplomacy. Undoubtedly Harold had been drinking: reason would be a blunt tool. Could I speak of my children's interests? Tell him how they can't sleep with volume so high. I had witnessed mean, nasty drunks relinquish their pool cues when Ben and Greg walked through the tavern door.

There was grinding of a starter motor, then an engine turning over. Sounds grew louder as headlights passed our window and then slowly faded in the distance. Quiet returned but only briefly.

The singer repeated the title of her song.

I observed through the window that Harold's truck was missing but the car with the tape deck played on. Covert action was the sensible option. I walked next door to the car, and because I had forgotten a flashlight I unsuccessfully fumbled with buttons and dials before finally disconnecting a wire leading to the cigarette lighter. Quiet again.

"What a jerk," I said in the direction of Julie as I slipped back into bed. "I'm going to ask Butters to have a talk with his help about rural etiquette."

She awoke and asked, "Is everything all right?"

I must have slept a short while before familiar noises again awakened me to the problem. An internal combustion engine. Quiet. A metal door slam. A wooden door slam. Voices coming from inside Butters's house. Again the wooden door slam. Brief silence preceded the now familiar singing voice.

Julie looked at her husband. Boys were whispering and probably listening for father's next move. I arose and walked to my dresser, where I picked out a neutral Western wardrobe: faded Lee Wranglers, a clean white Fruit of the Loom T-shirt with no logo, and Tony Lama boots with riding heels. Running shoes might have been a wiser choice.

I stepped out into the night. Both of Harold's vehicles were directly across the street. A dark figure was seated behind the steering wheel in the car with the driver's door ajar. An orange glow from a cigarette was visible through the windshield. Harold pivoted on the car seat, lowered his feet, and stood up in the road.

"Hey, Harold, would you mind turning the music down?"

He reached back into the car and pulled out a long dark object. I kept walking slowly toward him until he turned and I recognized a .22 caliber rifle pointing at me, held at hip level.

I gave my prepared statement, "Your music is keeping my boys from sleeping."

"Don't come close."

"You can understand that children need their sleep."

"This is loaded, and you're my prisoner."

"Let's be reasonable," I said, already knowing that wasn't in the cards. (Clichés rolled smoothly off my tongue.) I remember little of my side of the conversation but all of what he said.

"Stay where you are. You know you ain't got no right to touch my property, and there ain't no way you going to stop me playing my music." (Hearing double negatives still makes me nervous.)

"You're my prisoner."

Harold was drinking Bud. Rifle was bolt action with an open sight, similar to mine. A bullet through my midsection would enter and exit cleanly, with the possibility of perforating liver, kidneys, spleen, intestines . . . chance of nicking an artery or lodging in the spine. Should I try to wrestle the rifle away from him before or after the first shot?

Harold leaned back, resting on a fender, his right leg cocked with heel on a hub cap. The rifle was cradled. Was the safety on or off? His trigger finger was moist from the beer can. I developed a craving for my own can of Bud and asked my guard for permission. He nodded.

I turned (no sudden movement) and walked across the street through my gate and up to my back door, hesitated and called back to Harold, "Can I get you a fresh one?"

"Yeah, I could use 'nother."

Julie was standing in the kitchen directly under a bare light bulb and looking exceptionally pretty. I told her I had to go back out and humor Harold. "We'll never get to sleep if there's a madman taking potshots through the windows."

"Is everything all right?"

"No. Get my rifle, and I need two beers real quick. Don't worry; I'm not sure his rifle is even loaded. . . . Okay, here's my gun. Remember I showed you how to load? The bullets are on our truck dashboard. Go out the front door and don't slam it. He won't see you. I've got to go back and talk him down. . . . Also for safety put the kids on the floor under their bed, and when you've got the rifle loaded if Harold looks like he's going to shoot me, you shoot first. Aim at his head."

We could have simply called the county sheriff if I hadn't procrastinated on having a phone installed. A week ago I couldn't think of anyone I wanted to call.

I thought of spiking Harold's beer. Butters had once explained why he kept a bottle of Visine Eye Drops under the bar. "Little bit in a man's drink takes the fight right out of'm. Gives him the runs just like that. No cowboy's going to stay around with stink in his pants." Again I hadn't fully anticipated needs.

As I returned through my back gate, Harold reassumed the rifleman position. With his free hand he tapped on the fender where he wanted me to set his beer. Then I stepped backward to a neutral position in the center of the road, and he moved crablike over by the tailgate of his truck where he was shaded from starlight by an overhanging lilac bush. My eyes were readjusting to the night. I moved closer to hear better, though I needn't because he was only repeating the charge against me of violating his personal property. Then he added a second offense: home breaker.

"Lisa never would'a run away to a college if you hadn'ta brought those hippy students in. You're bad." He raised and lowered the rifle like a yardstick in the hand of a schoolmarm.

To plead my defense I stepped closer . . . probably over the line. I spoke generally of the innocence of intellectual temptations and the predictability of midlife crises. Harold said, "Shut up." I didn't have the opportunity to mention that Lisa was intelligent, sensitive, and well read before we arrived. She had given us back issues of the New Yorker and Gourmet long before I ever mentioned existentialism. She had always surprised me, like a truffle hidden in the shaded forest.

Lisa would reminisce about her interrupted studies at Bennington College; how she dropped out, married, and produced three children. Later when the marriage soured, and divorce was imminent, she made plans to return to college. But during the six-week waiting period for a divorce in Nevada, she met Warren. Soon she remarried and gave birth to a fourth child. College would have to wait at least until this son was high school age. By coincidence our arrival in Tuscarora coincided with her planned departure.

Harold may not have known these details. I kept my mouth shut.

Tammy Wynette sang on about having pride in your man, even though he's just a man.

Harold backed off as I stepped closer to hear him over the music. If Julie was watching, Harold and I must have been a curious couple, like an Italian attempting to speak with an Englishman: the former advancing to be close enough for conversation while the latter backpedals to maintain proper distance.

Tammy repeated that title once again.

Julie was probably lying in ambush under the aspen tree; frontierlike-wife with rifle butted to her shoulder; perhaps my sons huddled on each side clutching mother's long skirt and whispering low, "Now, Mom, now, now, shoot, c'mon shoot." (Urban television images.)

I didn't want Harold dead unless the situation deteriorated into him-or-me. He was slurring words and probably tiring as we closed in on a compromise: on Gold Street I would restrict myself to the north half and he would stay to the south. I would shut up on the issue of loud music being played at night and in return he would forego shooting me in the stomach. (I would have conceded more.)

I stepped forward again, thinking we should now shake hands, when Harold abruptly stumbled-backward-lowered-his-weapon-and-BOOM. The bullet must have ricocheted off the road between my feet. He deftly drew the bolt back, expelling a spent casing, and just as quickly had a fresh cartridge in the firing chamber. "The next one's for you." (Cliché now, but profound then.)

I listened for the report of return fire from across the street. I backed off in baby steps thinking that perhaps I was in Julie's line of fire. Tammy Wynette stopped singing. Quiet. Running shoes and war movies danced in my head: dart off in a crouched position, zigzag, dodge, and dive to safety behind a compost heap. I stood still listening before suggesting an armistice. "Why don't I just go and sit on my fence over there and you sit on your truck and we can discuss this?"

"Okay, 'cause nobody's goin' to take this gun away from me, least of all you."

I turned and saw Julie silhouetted in our doorway. She was empty-handed. Harold put his rifle back on the car seat.

"Is everything all right? The children are worried."

I replied, "I think so."

Harold grunted agreement, so I walked into my home where, for the few hours remaining before sunrise, I sat at the kitchen table drinking Budweiser. Physically, I was a catalog of symptoms: pale skin, weak legs, trembling fingers, incontinent bladder, and diarrhea.

"Of course, I tried to load your gun, but I guess I have forgotten how. I even tried to force one down the barrel but it wouldn't fit. Finally I just put the boys under their bed, like you told me. Then I sat on the bed facing the door. . . . I thought if Harold shot you and came into our house . . . maybe if he saw our gun I could scare him. Ben told me not to worry. He said, 'Dad's good at talking.'"

On Julie's next shopping trip to Elko she bought me a Tammy Wynette tape. "You'll feel better quicker when you have control over the music. Being dominated by another person has to be frightening."

Soon I was my normal self, though I credit my recovery more to Harold's quick departure from town than to any musical therapy.

In my mind, "What if?" played on a continuous loop. What if he had shot me? What if I had had a pistol in my back pocket? What if I had stayed in bed? What if I had had a bottle of Visine Eye Drops or a functioning telephone?

(Dry air can shrivel and twist vegetation. Could this low humidity and high altitude have a similar effect on humans?)

CHAPTER 3

Vegetables and Fish

City dwellers often plan two-week vacations in quest of blood sports and life-threatening adventures. Why else do they camp in bear-infested forests, kayak down rapids, and tie themselves together for assaults on mountain peaks? Countryside emigrants rarely relocate for such adrenalin-pumping excitement.

When I coaxed my family into moving high above pollution and population, gardening was in the back of my mind. There is a widely held belief that all life began in a garden. Historic records show bands of Shoshone and Paiute Indians migrating over these very mountains and camping in this valley. Their families feasted, or at least subsisted, on local plants, insects, fish, rodents, and, with occasional good fortune, a large ungulate. They crisscrossed high desert in patterns dictated by seasons. No archaeological evidence indicates that they cultivated any crops. Their world was a garden plot, and hunting and gathering was full-time, hard work.

In the late nineteenth century, equally industrious Euro-American emigrants attempted large-scale dry wheat farming and irrigated vegetable gardening in northeastern Nevada. Summers of drought withered those dreams of transforming this region into an Eden. Dedicated farmers moved farther west looking for California or Oregon, while others settled down, bought cowboy hats, and became cattle ranchers. Grass is perennial.

I wasn't planning to stake my livelihood on gardening. I fantasized only a small fenced plot cultivated to fulfill modest physical and spiritual goals. Cycles of effort followed by idleness. Most of my time was to be spent watching little plants grow bigger.

> It's amazing how easily and naturally the inner springs resume their functioning once you surrender to sheer idleness. (Henry Miller, *Big Sur and the Oranges of Hieronymus Bosch*, 102)

Also, I had a bad back from the poor posture of bending over a spinning potter's wheel. I trusted that the range of movement involved in gardening, the digging, raking, and weeding, might ameliorate some of the symptoms.

I selected seeds touted by catalogs to be precocious and tough: quick to maturity and frost hardy. My baby fruit trees and berry bushes arrived sealed in plastic wrap stamped with the guarantee "Good to thirty below zero." After I bought coils of water hose and an assortment of sprinkler heads, I thought I was prepared.

In *Living the Good Life*, Helen and Scott Nearing stress the importance of a cash crop. Theirs was maple syrup; mine would be pottery. Tuscarora could never attract many acquisitive tourists, but our family's wants were few. Over time a fiscal equilibrium established itself.

The processes involved in both gardening and pottery impose considerable down time: freshly thrown pots must dry a bit before being trimmed and more before being glazed and fired; in the garden even weeds need an undisturbed period to germinate. These respites allowed leisure time for me to explore in and around town and see what Nature was up to. Initially, I researched popular field guides to help identify the choice and edible from the nasty. Unfortunately these texts concentrated on plants growing in lush, humid climates. A few illustrations looked familiar, but black-and-white drawings gave this novice no confidence.

Fortunately my close neighbors were eager to teach.

"Have you seen those mushrooms coming up in the meadow?"

"No."

"You picked a mess of fuzzy britches yet?"

"No."

"Bushes up McCann full of chokecherries this year."

"Where?"

Knowledge of wild plants and topography of the area came as I examined samples on kitchen tables and watched maps being drawn on paper napkins. Nona, a widow, ex-miner, and ex-rancher, even told me the day and time when she would take me out and show me where everything was.

Three miles driving on dusty roads in an arc south and west of Tuscarora brought us to a halt at the edge of a step-over stream, McCann Crick.

"Boy, we're not fishing today, but there're some good holes . . . like there . . . back in those willows. Some morning you bring those boys of yours. All you need're worms. Won't bite on fancy bait."

Nona remained seated in the pickup shouting directions and pointing until I was standing by a mixed thicket of elderberry and chokecherry bushes. She noted that my trousers were entangled in primrose. "I'm going to show you what you do when the fish aren't biting."

Since none of the berries were ripe, she gave the approximate months when I should return to harvest and added very general instructions for making jam, wine, and tea. Before I walked back to the truck she pointed streamside to a patch of wild spearmint that she wanted picked.

NONA'S ELDERBERRY WINE

Loosely pack a clean clear-glass gallon jar with as many clusters of
ripe elderberries as will fit. Pour over these two quarts boiling water.
(Place jar in pan of warm water so that the boiling water won't break
it.) Cover with plastic wrap then screw on lid one and a half turns.
Set in a sunny place outside for three days or until all berries have
risen to top. Strain and squeeze through a jelly bag and return juice
to jar. Stir in 6 cups of sugar until dissolved, then 1 cup chopped
raisins. Cover lightly again and set in warm place inside for three
weeks. Strain through several thicknesses of cheesecloth and siphon
into clean sterilized wine bottles. Cork lightly and leave until there
are no small bubbles inside bottles. Cork tightly. Store for one year.

Nona's house in Tuscarora was constructed from recycled railroad
ties plastered over with white stucco and neatly trimmed in dark red.
She closely supervised its construction in the early 1950s. After selling
her ranch in the valley she wanted to retire to town. The lot is on the
southwest corner of Weed and Main Streets across from the Tuscarora
Tavern. Being at the busiest intersection, she could keep track of
comings and goings. In the afternoon, when her front yard was shaded,
she would sit on the porch and beckon passersby to join her. She was a
small woman with an oversized voice, like a VW Bug with a truck horn.
She always startled me. Rarely did she reminisce about ranching;
mostly Nona spoke of the mining days, occasionally surfacing to make
predictions. "You know, boy, the richest ore is still here, underground."

Her parents had moved from Iowa ("Ioway") before she could remember and settled in the boomtown of Goldfield, Nevada. Without
giving details, she described her youth as "frisky" and said her parents
were happy when she married young. Her husband was a youthful, unemployed miner from Cornwall, England. Goldfield's boom was over, so
the couple packed up and traveled to northeast Nevada, following rumors. The boom was also over here, but empty houses and abandoned

mining claims were tempting. This couple worked hard reopening a silver mine and discovering two rich deposits of mercury. Nona had five miscarriages during those mining years and no live births. After her husband died, she bought the ranch.

In retirement she now lived on income from leasing her mercury mines to a Colorado-based corporation that speculated on reopening when and if. The mines were never worked again, but her checks came regularly. Nona was also the sole owner of the Tuscarora Waterworks and assessed six dollars per month for each occupied house. The comings and goings of residents were a business interest.

The centerpiece of social life in Tuscarora was her three-handed pinocle game scheduled on Wednesday afternoons in her living room. When Nona reached eighty, she switched from normal playing cards to a large-print deck. As her vision continued to weaken, she began talk of suicide. "I won't do it in front of anyone, but got to do it while I can still see where the rifle is." Neighbors understood and henceforth dropped by to visit more often.

Names of her partners shuffled through the years because of untimely deaths and moves out of town. Della, who lived catty-corner across the intersection, was never a partner. Perhaps she begged off. She did have responsibilities as the proprietor of Rocks & Relics, her private museum filled with purple bottles, mining memorabilia, and nineteenth-century detritus. Occasionally an out-of-state car could be seen parked by the front door.

More likely, Nona didn't invite Della. These two women appeared to be about the same age, and both had lived in the valley longer than anyone else could remember. When they attended one of the infrequent social gatherings at the tavern, they smiled but sat apart.

Rumor was that Nona and Della shared a passion for one activity, "rubber necking," a term applied to the rural curious who listen in on all incoming telephone calls. Confirmation came from both women. Nona shouted as I walked by her yard, "Boy, there's somebody wants to talk to you from Illinois. Come on in, you can do your talking on my phone." Della told me of helping a worried mother down the valley who had received a call from her son in Portland, Oregon, telling of car trouble and needing money wired immediately. After the mother hung up she realized that she hadn't written down the name of her son's motel. She called Della. "Goodness, yes, Doris," Della replied, "He said the Clackmas Lodge just south of the city on route 205."

One summer after I was called over to sit on Nona's porch, she pointed across the intersection toward Della's museum and asked, "You ever notice that Della can be haughty? She's a little high and mighty for no reason. . . . She ever tell you about her first marriage? She won't. . . . Only lasted two weeks. . . . More like a long hayride than gettin' hitched."

The stretch of Main Street, downhill from the comfort of my home to a working studio, passes by the fence around Della's yard. We always waved, but on occasion she'd stand up from yard work and point to the gate. Any excuse was good enough for me to pause and procrastinate.

"You been visiting with Nona the other day? Sure kept you there a long time. . . . Likes to talk and gossip. . . . Guess you noticed that."

I nodded. Della was taller and more angular than Nona; and instead of gray hair, hers was dyed just a shade lighter than the bright orange poppies behind her. Her voice was soft.

"Nona's old now, but when she was a girl she was something. Would ride that horse of hers twenty miles over the mountains to Midas just to dance with strangers all night. My husband said he'd sure rather be her Bible rather'n her saddle."

Della turned and led me over to the base of a raised flower bed. "Look at these."

The wall caught my eye. It was cobbled together by Earl, her deceased, second husband, who was an acquisitive rock hound: chunks of purplish-brown petrified wood dominated, accented by green malachite coursed through with veins of bright blue azurite. The corners were braced with boulders of red cinnabar ore, the color of dried blood. (This brought to mind one of her displays under glass in the museum— the angry pistol used in our town's first murder.) Delicate green foliage intertwined with the orange flowers above.

"Nona never told you about her second husband? Didn't think so. He was so much younger . . . a gambler. Stayed with her just long enough, then he was gone."

I asked where the poppies came from.

"China! Those railroad coolies brought the seeds. Celestials had to have their dope. Down back of your kilns they had special houses where they smoked. All burned down after they left."

Poppies are spectacular when one comes upon orange bouquets growing wild among sagebrush and weeds; and if newcomers ask me, I repeat Della's story of the seeds' provenance. Doubters site color photos from National Geographic or Smithsonian illustrating endless fields of white opium poppies flourishing in Southeast Asia. I shrug my shoulders.

After Della passed away, a delegation of Hell's Angels, leather clad, sleeveless, and tattooed, drove in on motorcycles and stopped long enough to harvest every poppy pod visible from the street. These gleaners were believers, and as further proof, they returned the following year.

In Della's garden there was also an oversized patch of day lilies. She handed me a shovel and escorted me. "Dig as many roots as you want. Plant them in the sun away from poppies and give them lots of water. Too much water'll kill poppies." She said that both the roots and the blossoms of day lilies can be eaten: raw, boiled, or roasted. There is no distinctive flavor, but the flowers add color on top of a salad or floating in a soup. To thicken a stew, roots or dried blossoms can be the substitute for okra, one of many plants that won't grow well here. Before serving my family, I looked for confirmation in Euell Gibbons's Stalking the Wild Asparagus.

D. P.'S CUCUMBER SOUP WITH DAY LILIES

4–6 servings

Melt 3 tbsp. butter or margarine in a large Dutch oven. Add ½ cup of minced onion and 2 minced garlic cloves. Cook until onions are transparent, then add 1½–2 lbs of cucumbers peeled and cut into ½-inch sections, 6 cups of chicken broth, 2 tsp. wine vinegar, 1 tsp. tarragon, and 25 dry day lily flowers. Bring to a boil then stir in 4 tbsp. couscous, farina, or grits. Simmer for half an hour, then blend in a food mill. Salt and pepper to taste. Serve either hot, warm, or cold with a single fresh blossom of day lily floating in each bowl.

Another neighbor, Louie the Frenchman, introduced me to wild rhubarb, which grows in backyards and on abandoned lots. He led me behind his house and into a waist-high jungle of giant leaves. He reminisced about carrying root stock in his pack while prospecting, and when he believed he'd discovered an ore body he'd pitch his tent and plant rhubarb nearby. Before the next move, he would dig out a few roots to take along. According to Louie, today's hikers could still stumble onto plants growing wild near an abandoned camp.

Louie immigrated from France early in this century, and Nona still referred to him affectionately as "Frenchie." Her belief was that he had hidden out in this country to avoid being drafted for World War I. He never found much gold and had subsisted mostly by shooting stray cattle that had evaded the branding iron. (Miners call these yearlings "oreanas" and considered them to be wild game. Ranchers disagreed.)

Louie cut an armload of his rhubarb for Julie, and as he was breaking off the leaves he warned, "Don't ever eat these. Only billy goats can do it without sickening. Don't know why they're tougher than us." I was invited to return and gather roots for transplanting. " Don't know why you have to wait till the stalks die back to dig'm. . . . Just the way things are."

Julie caught a foraging spirit after next-door neighbor Butters drove her on a field trip gathering fuzzy britches (referred to in texts as dwarf waterleaf or *Hydrophyllaceae*). Later she attempted to lead a family expedition but had forgotten where that particular lush canyon was; still she remembered how to identify: short plants with delicate violet blossoms clustered at the base of the stem and small fuzzy green leaves. We hiked around and up to a clearing that had been burned in a range fire the previous summer, and we picked enough to share.

This plant with a generic green leafy flavor was part of the Indian diet and may be served raw in salad or steamed for a side dish. The spring harvest is short. From the day they can be identified until they die off is less than a month, but fortunately this parallels the edible life cycle of dandelion greens. These two are natural partners.

PARKS'S DOUBLE WILD WILTED SALAD

1 quart scissored fuzzy britches
1 quart torn dandelions
6 strips bacon cut into ½-inch sections (⅓ cup virgin olive oil
    may be a healthy substitute, but not recommended)
3 teaspoons honey
⅓ teaspoon dry yellow mustard
¼ cup garlic or balsamic vinegar

A. Wash greens well before tearing and scissoring.
B. Fry bacon pieces slowly until crisp.
C. Add remaining ingredients into frying pan and stir for a
    minute or two.
D. Pour from frying pan into a ceramic salad bowl filled with
    greens and toss briefly.
E. Serve while still warm.

Alexander H. Smith's *Mushroom Hunter's Field Guide* gave me confidence to take that first bite into a wild mushroom. For the next twenty-four hours I monitored my bodily functions closely, digestive tract and nervous system, for any symptoms of poisoning. The next day I felt safe serving the family a side dish of mushrooms sautéed in butter. Three neighbors had also inspected these mushrooms and agreed with Smith's recommendation of "edible and choice." Nona even pointed to the tiny animal teeth marks on the edge of one mushroom as a good sign they might be non-poisonous.

Mushrooms don't pop up in this area very regularly, only occasionally in hayfields bordering the Owyhee River. If a freak rainstorm is followed by several days of balmy weather, we will drive down and search; precipitation and temperature must be perfectly coordinated. Normally when a soaking rain reaches the valley it is followed by a cold front.

We pick only "meadow mushrooms" (*Agaricus campestis*), which are very similar to the common supermarket variety and fortunately very dissimilar to the deadly poisonous *Aminitas* family with scary names like "panther fungus" or "destroying angel." Smith fosters caution against *Aminitas*, "The symptoms are delayed, making the application of first aid almost useless." Death follows.

Agaricus c. is the only fungi I can identify, therefore the only one I gather. A tiny brown unappealing mushroom thrives on the topside of decaying cowpies, and urban visitors have speculated that this one may be hallucinogenic, but it hasn't been sampled in my presence.

In those rare years when mushrooms are abundant we bring home grocery sacks full, spread them out on a table in the studio, and start slicing the caps into strips. These are strung on thread like popcorn or cranberries and hung up to dry behind the wood stove; long banners loop up and down from the edge of bookshelves. Later they can be stored in lidded buckets and will retain rich flavor for years.

Piñon pine nuts were a staple for Native Americans, but the closest stand of these trees is about a hundred miles south of Tuscarora. Back to Nature must have limits: for gathering, line of sight establishes a perimeter for me. In this valley that distance is approximately ten miles. I make exceptions for fishing expeditions. Julie is less rigid. Her friend Inez was a survivalist with no limits, who stored fifty-pound sacks of beans and corn, dozens of candles, and other miscellaneous items that might be needed when The End is near. This bunker was under her home in Elko, but she came to visit us often, bringing five-gallon plastic buckets filled with more berries or fruit or vegetables than Julie could deal with. "We've got to stock up, got to stock up," was the cry.

One fall Inez decided that we all needed to hoard pine nuts. I mentioned that a pound of the processed seeds, though expensive, costs less than a tank full of gasoline. She planned to gather at least fifty pounds.

Descendants of the Shoshone and Paiute tribes have hereditary rights to pick what they need before the rest of us are allowed to gather any. Inez obtained the necessary permit from the U.S. Forest Service, and with this in her pocket and an aluminum ladder and two gunnysacks in the bed of our pickup, the two women drove south.

Inez was vague about exactly where, between Carlin and Eureka, she had seen piñon trees beside the highway. So they had to stop several times and hike over to check out a suspicious stand. From a distance, cedar trees caused confusion. Once they found a grove of the proper trees, but Indians had stripped the branches clean.

Late that afternoon these two stumbled into a canyon and onto untouched piñon pines. Taking turns, one of them would climb the ladder while the other stood below holding an open sack. Two full sacks was all they could handle along with the ladder as they retraced their trail uphill to the pickup. At the edge of the road Julie suddenly realized that she had forgotten her purse with the truck key. They packed their load in the pickup bed before turning around and walking back down the canyon. Finally as the tree shadows lengthened Julie found her purse. She told me later, "It's uncanny how all piñon pine trees look alike."

Townsfolk were relieved when just before dark they saw our truck returning to Tuscarora. These were not two women you'd welcome home with bear hugs: they appeared from a distance dustier than rodeo bull riders, and on close inspection they were stickier than small girls after eating cotton candy. They were lacquered in pine resin. The door handles and the steering wheel were as tacky as flypaper. Inez brought a bottle of cooking oil out from the kitchen, "The only solvent I know of for this stuff."

While the women cleaned up, the rest of us, family and students, got sticky loading pine cones onto pans for the oven. Low heat allowed the cones to open and free the nuts. An aroma of Athens filled the kitchen. Memories of retsina kept me mellow as I cracked the hard little kernels and freed the small seeds. For extravagant snacks we ate these raw and at mealtimes tossed a modest handful into a fresh green salad. No experiments were made to dry them further to grind into flour. In no time ours were eaten while Inez took her share for storage in the Elko bunker.

The capriciousness of Nature untamed was to be balanced by produce from my cultivated garden. A gardener should plant only what will grow well in his climate and varieties that the family relishes. Prudence demands a garden sized to your needs: only plant as much as you can consume fresh, store, or share with neighbors and animals. This was impossible to precisely calculate because I couldn't predict the appetite of wild ground squirrels and deer. I overplanted.

Insects are also unpredictable predators, but because of our winters, they are not always a problem here. In three- to four-year cycles grasshoppers swarm through the valley like the army of Tamerlane pillaging. After experiencing the first invasion I prepared for their return by constructing a second fence around the garden, three feet inside the existing barrier. This buffer zone was patrolled by a dozen Peking ducks—renowned for their fondness for insects, for guile and voraciousness.

During the insect-free years, feeding an army of ducks with expensive commercial grain was a burden on our peacetime economy. Absent an enemy the ducks turned their attentions to sex. Initially I gathered a few eggs but learned that neither boiling nor frying altered their rubbery, unappealing texture. The rest of the eggs were allowed to remain in rudimentary ground nests, go to term, and hatch.

Of course we ate ducks as they matured and before a new generation could begin reproducing itself, but Nature was too profligate. I posted a sign on the outside fence: FREE DUCKS. Neighbors hesitated until I promised to deliver dead birds, plucked, gutted, and oven ready. Next-door neighbor Butters, a fly fisherman, dropped over and requested that I separate and save certain neck feathers for him.

Price of feed and boring labor drove me to an armistice with grass-hoppers. I would sacrifice a portion of my crop to insects every few years and accept this as a tithe to a cycle of Nature: a rosy view of defeat, from my compromised prospective. I had always hoped to appear rational while I was learning to live in the country. My old friends and blood relatives might stop writing or calling if they believed I had stepped too far over the line.

The selection of seeds for the garden was not quite as rational as stated earlier. Julie and I sat opposite each other at the kitchen table, separated by a stack of catalogs. I weeded through the glossy advertise-ments searching for companies headquartered high in the Rockies or low in a dry desert. The number of days from planting to picking must match our short growing season, and the plants must not be heavy drinkers. I circled the absolute quickest growing varieties.

Opposing me sat Julie turning pages, smiling indiscriminately at il-lustrations and underlining such long-season, humidity-loving plants as tomatoes, okra, field corn, crowder peas, cucumbers, pole beans, and watermelon. She even circled a peach tree! All were flashbacks to a happy childhood in the Piedmont of North Carolina. Obligingly, I expanded plans for my practical garden to include her nostalgia corner.

In order to not waste time hauling manure, I had chosen the aban-doned cattle corral for my garden, but preparation of this soil slowed me down. Primitive tools were all I had: pick, digging bar, hoe, and shovel. The top six inches of dry, well-aged cow manure was wonderfully light and friable, but underneath was a hardpan of earth compacted through years of hoofbeats by half-ton steers. Our first garden should have been smaller.

Nona visited during this stage of soil preparation and, noting the size of the plot, asked whether I planned to turn Tuscarora into a meadow.

"Goin' to take a lot'a water."

I tried to placate her by explaining that I had no plans to plant the entire field. The perimeter had been freed of weeds only to allow me a clear shot at advancing rodents and rabbits. She nodded and left, but checked by at regular intervals during growing season. Occasionally in the heat of late summer she would declare a moratorium on sprinklers. Only hand watering was allowed until the spring above town picked up.

With experience, we further reduced garden size. Julie passed through her sentimental stage after observing how slowly Southern plants mature at high altitude. Julie's tomatoes and cucumbers now thrive indoors in large flowerpots. I learned to rid the garden of weeds by watering the soil, then covering it for two weeks with sheets of black plastic. All undesirable seeds germinate and are easily hoed before the garden is planted. Another inspiration came regarding where to deposit seeds in rows: in dry country you don't plant on the hills you have made but in the valleys where water will collect. Literature on gardening presumes frequent cloudbursts and gully washers, and therefore authors recommend hill planting. I was slow to deviate.

Our shopping list for seeds became predictable. At the top of the page were root crops (potatoes, beets, and turnips) followed by members of the kohlrabi family (broccoli, brussels sprouts, and cabbage). And, of course, squash grows abundantly. I consider this a hostile vegetable because it turns neighbor against neighbor in a late summer fury to give and not receive. Except for squash and potatoes the flavor of these vegetables improves after a nip of frost. For salads we regularly plant short rows of rapidly maturing greens along with onions and radishes: a tough garden tolerant of Tuscarora's vicissitudes—Nature and Nona.

Hoeing and spading in fertile soil inevitably uncovers earthworms. As I work my way down a row, robins often flutter and land behind me then quickly fly home to their nests to feed a brood. I also gather my share in a can, which I later top off with kitchen scraps to keep them wiggly until my next fishing adventure. I imagine myself fishing once every week. Studio routine and arrivals of unexpected visitors often distract. Once a month is a rule.

Wild Horse, Wilson, or Willow Creek—roll the dice—all are reservoirs within an hour's drive of Tuscarora. When time is a constraint, McCann Creek, Rock Creek, or the Owyhee River is closer. Bass, catfish, and crappie are menu possibilities, though I generally cast into the waters for trout: brookies, rainbow, brown, or cutthroat. I could boast the length and weight of individual fish, but such data are unreliable. Lying is as integral to fishing as swearing is to a barroom pool game.

Julie doesn't share my enthusiasm for weaving a path through willow branches on a stream bank or sitting for hours on a hard, flat rock lakeside. She's particularly reticent to accompany me when I am bundled in goose down, planning to spend hours standing by a six-inch hole in the ice of a frozen reservoir. With our ears covered by caps and hoods and the wind blowing, conversation is infrequent. I relish the quiet and the idleness: Julie becomes preoccupied with thoughts of chores she could be doing at home. I contemplate whether or not I should change bait, or perhaps switch location and drill a fresh hole. I stare at the rod tip speculating whether the twitching is caused by the breeze or a trout's nibbling. Fishing can seem boring, though as an outdoor activity it is less like work than gardening.

Our diet is rich in fish protein. Smaller trout I pan fry.

GINGER TROUT TUSCARORA FOR EIGHT
In a brown paper bag place 2 large handfuls flour and an equal amount of cornmeal plus salt and pepper to taste. Shake trout individually in the mixture until well coated. Place on a newspaper.

In a cast iron skillet fry trout in ½ cup olive oil, ¼ cup bacon grease, and ¼ cup butter until fish are golden brown. Place on a ceramic platter in warm oven. Save grease in pan.

While trout are frying make the following mixtures in separate ceramic bowls:

    2 cloves garlic, crushed
    48 strokes of grated fresh gingerroot
    ¼ cup honey
    3 tablespoons cider vinegar
    Slightly less than ½ cup soy sauce

    ——

    2 tablespoons cornstarch
    ¾ cup water

On low heat add #1 mixture to the skillet in which the fish were fried. Cook for about five minutes, then slowly stir in #2 until smooth and thickened. Serve in a separate ceramic bowl for your guests to ladle onto trout as desired. Chopped scallions may be sprinkled on top as decoration.

Trout too large to fit in a skillet are cooked over charcoal and most often eaten without a sauce. The whole fish with head intact (cheeks are tender morsels) is brushed generously with bacon grease or olive oil before being placed on the grill. Twigs of fresh sagebrush may be added to the coals for a smokier flavor.

Large fish should cook for seven to ten minutes on each side and be brushed frequently inside and out with more grease or oil. I remove trout from the fire and arrange them on a very large stoneware platter; each will serve three or four guests with normal appetites.

Fish are touted as a healthful alternative to red meat. Other medical reasons justify some regularity in going fishing. To my skeptical wife, a former nurse, I insist that a few hours waterside with rod and reel lowers my blood pressure ten points both systolically and diastolically. The Reverend Sun Myung Moon, an avid fisherman, has stated that his purpose is not to catch fish but to get closer to God. Respectfully I stand with the opposing camp whose mission is to catch a limit while keeping the Almighty at arms' length. That eternal embrace shall come soon enough.

Tuscarora Cemetery.

The town lies in

the background.

CHAPTER 4   Minerals: Dust to Dust

In a cavern, in a canyon / Excavating for a mine /
Dwelt a miner, Forty-niner, / And his daughter Clem-en-tine.

Oh my dar-ling, oh my dar-ling, / Oh my dar-ling Clem-en-tine! /
Thou art lost and gone for-ev-er / Dreadful sor-ry, Clem-en-tine!
—POPULAR NINETEENTH-CENTURY MINING SONG

Names and dates chiseled on tombstones are facts. The epitaphs are not,
but may be a more telling story of Tuscarora.

ANNIE
Wife of
B. J. BYRNE
Died
April 6, 1905
Aged 25 yrs.
Gone but not forgotten
——

MOTHER
Julia Ann Wardrop
Warren Co. Ind.
Jan. 1, 1843
Mar. 27, 1905
ONLY SLEEPING

——

In
Loving Memory
of
Mortimer A. Curieux
Beloved Husband of
Lillian M. Curieux
Died Dec. 23, 1906
Aged 26 Yrs.
Sheltered and Safe from Sorrow

——

AT REST
S. L. STARR
Native of Wisn
DIED
May 6, 1883
Aged 31 YEARS

Other markers attest to diverse homelands:

Gottardo Pattani
Born
April 7, 1865
Died
Aug. 12, 1902
Native of Giornico

Switzerland
FATHER
—

In
Memory of
DENNIS LINEHAN
A native of
County Cork, Ireland
DIED
Sept. 11, 1878
Aged 41 Yr's.
—

FATHER
In memory of
WILLIAM TREMBATH
Beloved husband
Native of
Cornwall, England
Born
May 18, 1842
Died July 12, 1902
—

John Lugio
DIED
Aug. 11, 1904
Native of Flores
Portugal
—

NIEVE INCHAUSTY
Y. URIZAR
Fallecio dia 17 de Enero
De 1915 Edad dos a os
NIÑA

Grieving families must have doubted the decision to settle in a remote godforsaken spot far from hospitals, relatives, and friends. The romantic image of a lone prospector with his gold pan and pick tied to a burro stumbling onto a fortune is a twentieth-century fantasy. Life appears to have been unfair, mean, and unduly short, particularly for children:

In Memory Of
Arthur Kendrick
Died Sept 22, 1894
Age 4 days
—

John Allen Pollock
Dec 15, 1893
Dec 16, 1893
—

OSCAR GEORGE
infant son of
Geo. C. & Ivy M.
FAIRCHILD
June 22, 1894
June 14, 1896
Bye, Bye
Baby Oscar

All patterns in life may be cyclical, but they become particularly noticeable in the boom and bust of mining communities. Sorrow, greed, and lies rose closely behind dreams and optimism. The history of Tuscarora recorded in books and articles was researched from archives of nineteenth-century newspapers and interviews with the progeny of settlers.

It is unlikely that in the nineteenth century the *Tuscarora Times-Review* or the *Elko Independent* were any more accurate than our newspapers are today.

From listening to old-timers ramble on, and to present-day geologists pitch their stories, I have to conclude that mining buffs exaggerate the past and future: both tonnage extracted and the riches still beneath the ground.

Lies about the West—lies that are projected every day in vivid color on a big screen somewhere—have a potency with the public that their modest truths can rarely match.
—LARRY MCMURTRY, New York Review of Books, October 22, 1998

Although I distrust the veracity of written and oral histories of Tuscarora, I cannot resist citing some clippings to add a palpable Western flavor.

Tuscarora Times-Review, February 20, 1888

> In 1867 Tuscarora was discovered as a placer mining camp by Stephen and John Beard, who made up a party consisting of eight or nine persons, for the purpose of examining the mineral outlook in northeastern Nevada. . . . These gentlemen were induced to make this trip of explorations from information derived from several Indians. . . . The party started from Austin and headed for the Humboldt Valley, arriving there about the first of July, having been attracted there by the report of a rich copper mine. They were met there by Captain Jim Johnson, an Indian, who told them he could show them better mines, pointing towards Tuscarora. . . . [They] arrived at what is now known as Old Tuscarora on the 11th day of July 1867. . . . [G]old was discovered to exist and a number of locations were made. . . . [T]he Beard brothers proceeded to locate a water right and build a water ditch from McCann Creek, some three miles to the diggings, which is south of Tuscarora today.

Mining and Scientific Press, October 31, 1868

> Tuscarora received its name on the 10th of July, 1867, a short time after the discovery on McCann creek. S.M. Beard Hamilton McCann,

William Heath, C.M. Benson, Jacob Maderia, Charles Gardner, A.M. Berry and John Hovendon . . . held a meeting for the purpose of organizing a district. When it came to giving it a name, Charley Benson suggested that it be called after the United States gunboat Tuscarora. (ed. This was the ship he had served on during the Civil War).

Reese River Reveille, April 15, 1868

John Higgins, who recently returned to this city from McCann creek, Tuscarora district, in the Goose Creek country, does not give a very favorable account on the yield of the placer mines there. After sluicing for a week he found his earnings to be less than a dollar a day, and he concluded it would not pay to continue the business. But gold bearing quartz ledges are still believed to be profitable.

Elko Independent, October 23, 1870

Charley Drumm came in from his ranch in Independence valley this week. He reports quite a population at Tuscarora, consisting of about 125 China men and twenty to thirty whites. There is one American store and one China store at Tuscarora. The water having dried up, the Chinese are packing dirt to water, and some of them are making considerable money. One China company has taken out . . . $5,000. from dirt packed on their bamboo sticks. Most of the claims are owned by the Chinese, having been purchased . . . from the original white locaters. These claims pay well, from $5 to $10 to $20 per day, during the rainy season. Mr. Drumm says one nugget of 25 ounces was found last Spring—another of 15 ounces, and several pieces of four to five ounces. The Chinese are constantly accumulating in the valley, and probably next Winter there will be not less than 500 of them. It is very liberal on the part of Uncle Sam to furnish these placers to the Chinese free of charge, while half the white people of Nevada are too poor to buy a poll tax receipt to get to the polls.

Mining and Scientific Press, March 18, 1876

> There are at present about 60 white men in the camp and about the same number of China men. The town consists of about 20 houses, two hotels, two stores, one lodging house, one blacksmith shop, one barber shop, one butcher shop, and three or four saloons. . . . It is a very poor place for men to come to in search of employment, there being too many here at present for what work there is to be done.

Disappointed Euro-American miners became prospectors again in their spare time, sampling rock outcrops and gravel beds in the hills adjacent to Old Tuscarora. In 1871 wide veins of silver ore were discovered two miles northeast, and within a year, settlement of the present day Tuscarora began: buildings hauled in by teams of oxen, tents pitched, businesses relocated, and a maze of shafts and adits dug. (More than fifty miles of collapsing tunnels are estimated to exist under town.)

Engineering and Mining Journal, July 29, 1876

> A rich strike is reported in this mine (the Grand Prize) . . . an old location made in May 1875. . . . Some eighteen or twenty tons of rich ore from the new bonanza has been forwarded to the Leopard mill at Cornucopia for reduction, but the result to the workings has not yet been made public.

Northeastern Nevada Historical Society Quarterly, summer and fall 1971

> The question of accurate reporting of the State's mineral production is not new. The existence of a bullion, a severance, tax led to some elaborate methods of tax evasion in the 1870's and later.

Report of the Surveyor General and State Land Register of the State of Nevada for the Years 1879 and 1880

> The difficulty of obtaining correct reports from County Assessors has always been one of the sorest afflictions of the Surveyor General. The

hair of my respected predecessor turned gray while battling for the desired statistics; the present incumbent has already become bald . . . and now declares in favor of a "stronger government," as applied to County Assessors. . . . There are fourteen assessors, and their reports show just fourteen degrees of competency; from utter stupidity to admirable ability.

YEAR	ASSESSOR'S FIGURE	REPORTED SHIPMENTS
1878	$1,107,797	$1,212,336
1881	156,000	422,000
1882	350,000	544,000
1883	486,000	662,000
1885	178,000	333,000
1887	183,000	285,000
1888	565,000	690,000

Northeastern Nevada Historical Society Quarterly, 1971

The decade between 1880 and 1890 saw Tuscarora reach its highest estimated population of approximately 2,500 (in 1888) and begin the decline that stretched slowly through the 1890's. After 1900, the transition from a mining camp to a ranching and distributing center was complete.

Tuscarora Times-Review, May 29, 1900

Last week twenty-five Japs came up from San Francisco to work on the railroad at Brown's Station, Nevada. An American who saw them get off the train commenced to kick about the importation of foreign labor. An Irishman who works at the gravel pit, just below town, turned to him and said, "Yez is an American, but who doog the canals uv the country but furriners? Who built the railroads uv the country but furriners? And who the devil discoovered the coontry but furriners."

Tuscarora Cemetery. Most plots are fenced, in the custom of the nineteenth century. It is a poignant sign of the town's abrupt decline that many large plots, obviously intended for several generations of a family, include only a single grave. Photo by Al Higgins.

Northeastern Nevada Historical Society Quarterly, summer and fall, 1971

The ditches [in Old Tuscarora] were reportedly abandoned in 1900, the year of Stephen M. Beard's death. The last Chinese miner died in 1927. In 1934, boys playing near his home uncovered a cache of dust and nuggets valued at $1200.

Through her living room window, Nona witnessed a hearse removing the last coffin from the Chinese section of the Tuscarora Cemetery in the early 1950s. These remains were then shipped to Taiwan for traditional interment. A half-dozen crumbling stone foundations are all that mark old Tuscarora. Twentieth-century treasure and bottle hunters have sifted and resifted the surrounding debris.

In the 1970s, a tourist drove into town and parked his motor home in front of the tavern. When Butters came out and walked over to talk, the visitor was unloading his long-handled metal detector and spoke first. "Bet you don't see one of these around here very often."

Butters stopped and blew his nose. "Well, probably no more often than once a week."

After the Dexter Mine closed in 1903, the digging around Tuscarora was sporadic, done mostly by treasure-hunting tourists. Of course every few years the silhouette of a drilling rig boom might be sighted on the horizon, but in a few weeks it would disappear. Exploration geologists are forever optimistic in an area that has previously been mined.

> It's a paradise for geologists, of course, because the geology [of northeastern Nevada] is extremely complex. . . . This is challenging for a geologist. . . . A fascinating area to work in. (John Livermore, geologist, in *Tuscarora*, directed by David Schickele, produced by Kim Shelton, 1989)

But, as we were to discover, Tuscarora was no paradise when a mine is reactivated. Modern miners are mostly truck drivers. In May 1984, after the earth had warmed enough for my seedlings to be planted outside, I was distracted by truck engines and the churning of drills burrowing into the ground. Noise was concentrated south of town beyond the Glory Hole, our deep, watery reminder of the Dexter Mine.

Standing on the cliff above the water, looking down, I saw a large-mouth black bass surface for insects, and there beyond the water's far edge, the dark, greasy boom of a drill. Of course, noise is natural for a machine, but it seemed out of place that day.

Within a week the sounds grew more annoying, closer to home. I smelled fumes from a rig in the center of Main Street between the hotel and Nona's home, and I saw a second down Weed Street in front of Jerry and Dede's. I telephoned De and learned that she had spoken with the drillers. They were just following orders from their boss, Pecos Resources Ltd., a Canadian company that had leased the mineral rights under Tuscarora. In Nevada such an arrangement allows private companies to explore regardless of who owns the surface.

By June, parallel green rows were visible in my garden, and Pecos was continuing to drill what appeared to be a random pattern of holes in our streets and yards. The workers drove into town and began their shift at dawn, then continued rumbling until sunset, when they drove away.

Julie contacted a lawyer in Elko, who explained the seriousness of our predicament: the original plat map of Tuscarora had disappeared from the courthouse vault sometime in the late 1930s. Because the population was sparse, the county commissioners considered it a ghost town and never resurveyed. The quit claim deeds that each of the townsfolk had received at the time they purchased their homes were valid. The lawyer tried to reassure Julie. The fact that the county assessor continued to mail us property tax bills implied our surface rights; but if the issue were to go to trial, we should realize that the state constitution was written by miners. Mineral extraction is still considered to be the highest use of Nevada's land. We were advised to remain patient, wait and see. "Perhaps they won't find anything."

De's husband, Jerry, drove truck for a mine, but an operation twenty miles away in a wilderness on the far side of the Independence Mountains. Not in our front yard. He opposed the idea of being employed closer to home, and from his experience he advised the town, "We better watch out. This Pecos operation looks serious."

De and Julie drove to Elko on several occasions to research courthouse records hoping to document our property rights. Later Julie spoke by phone with a discouraged state historian in Carson City, "Modern mining . . . I don't know whether it's worse or ranks number two to vandalism."

Fall came in 1984, my clue to harvest beets and brussels sprouts; but I was wondering whether it was worthwhile for Julie to take the trouble to freeze them. She and De became more optimistic about the future after they put together a package of historical documents, yellowed deeds and newspaper clippings, and testimonials from old-timers—all attesting to a unique significance for what was left of historic Tuscarora. This trove of evidence was presented to the county commissioners in petitioning them to grant the town "historical status." Julie and De believed roadside plaques might impede progress.

The commission was composed of retired ranchers, real estate salesmen, and small businessmen: cowboy boots and bola ties. They examined the collected documents and listened patiently. Then they unanimously voted, "No." The chairman explained to citizens that the wording of the applicable Nevada statute explicitly states that historical preservation should never stand in the way of mining.

The mining revival was disruptive for a reclusive community: neighbors were forced to congregate and to work together. Normally, trying to unify Tuscarora was like loading frogs into a wheelbarrow. Uncertainty had a calming effect. We had no allies among local elected officials. We were wary of the outsiders who drove in very slowly and unannounced: there were geologists disguised as friendly college professors, unemployed blue-collars who spoke in double negatives, and business types who exited cars with tinted windows and walked our streets shod in Gucci loafers.

One morning a clipping was pinned on the post office bulletin board. Pecos had invested over $1 million in exploration but would hold off actual mining for at least ninety days; no reason stated. This bit of newsprint gradually yellowed during the next three years. Would they start mining soon or would they go away? No one made long-term plans.

April 1987: "The Tuscarora Mine" was an item on the county commissioners' agenda. Tuscarora residents packed the gallery, as best twelve people could. The president of a mining company called Fischer-Watt, based in Reno, stood at the podium and announced that his company would commence open-pit mining south of Tuscarora just as soon as the Glory Hole could be pumped dry. (I noted that he, too, was wearing a bola tie and cowboy boots.)

Below where the president stood was a scale model on a long table, depicting the future south side of Tuscarora after mining had ceased and reclamation been completed: a cerulean blue lake (to be a hundred feet deep, three hundred feet north to south and nine hundred feet east to west), encircled by mature willow trees in fall colors. The low hills in the background would be created from waste rock and gravel. These stage promontories had been sprayed a poisonous chrome green, presumably to signify grass. The president concluded his talk by promising that no homes in Tuscarora would be "impacted." We raised our hands. All questions received similar, Panglossian answers. No one clapped. Utopian ideas frightened us.

By the time dump trucks and bulldozers arrived in Tuscarora, London gold prices had risen to $446 per ounce. I declined an invitation to stand on the cliff above as the Glory Hole was pumped out, though some neighbors did and then descended into the shallow water to net bass. Before mud had enough time to dry and crack, small holes were drilled, and dynamiting began.

Before my garden sprouted that summer, Fischer-Watt had resold the mine to Horizon Gold Shares, a newly formed company based in Golden, Colorado. Soon the president, John Watson, arrived in Tuscarora to meet with residents. According to him, any friction between the company and the town could be worked out amicably if only we kept out lawyers, the media, and the Sierra Club. Unwittingly, but clearly, he had mapped out our strategy.

The change of ownership was hardly noticed at first: tremors from blasting had the same intensity as did the roar of new trucks going forward and the dinging when they reversed. Dust still permeated the community. Soon rumors were circulating that Watson planned to widen the pit toward town. A few homes would have to be "impacted." More rumors followed.

During deer season in the fall, it is common to see neighbors driving around with rifles silhouetted in racks on the rear windows of their pickup trucks. The mine manager complained that his workers were fearful because they had heard that a drill helper with Fischer-Watt had been shot off his rig by a sniper. When I laughed, the manager summoned the sheriff, who came out from Elko and drove slowly one lap around town.

Watson assigned this manager the task of acquiring property from the residents in town. He walked nervously from door to door offering embarrassingly low prices to purchase homes. Only two absentee owners accepted through the mail. Horizon needed more area to dig. The following summer the manager was quoted in the *Sacramento Bee*, "The people are, for lack of a better word, squatters. . . . It's patented ground. We own it" (July 7, 1989).

The reporter from the *Sacramento Bee* was a late arrival. The first one had come from Elko; then reinforcements joined from Reno, Salt Lake City, San Francisco, Boston, and New York City. To locals it was the sound of friendly hoofbeats; to the reporters it was a race to stake their claim to a human interest bonanza. One of them remarked, "Here is a modern day David and Goliath story."

A video company from San Francisco began production of an hour-long feature. Shooting took place at intervals over the next fourteen months. The Sierra Club of Reno telephoned its moral support and, toward the end of Horizon's occupation, sent us information on how to apply to the secretary of the interior for a future ban on surface mining within a five-mile radius of town.

CBS Evening News with Dan Rather, August 7, 1989, report by John Blackstone

D.R. The finest fantasy living above veins of gold could mean great riches for some. It's also a story of great foreboding facing the loss of the old homestead. The fantasies and the fears come together in one Western community. John Blackstone has been there.

J.B. Through one hundred and twenty years of boom and bust, Tuscarora, Nevada, has refused to die, but now its twenty-five residents worry the town will be devoured by the same thing that gave it life—a gold mine.

The threat to Tuscarora is part of a new gold rush that has more than doubled the production in the U.S. in the past three years, but it is more destructive than any gold rush that has gone before. [The sounds and a view of explosions in the background.]

Today gold seekers are blasting enormous pits and crushing tons of rock. They're looking for microscopic specks. Huge piles of crushed ore are sprinkled with cyanide which soaks through the tons of earth for one ounce of gold. But the battle for Tuscarora is also a classic Wild West showdown—the miners versus the settlers.
The Horizon Gold Company says the town's people are no more than squatters. Legally it's unclear who owns the land; a judge may have to decide. But Nevada law lets almost nothing stand between miners and their gold.

Tuscarorans say the mine is destroying Nevada's history; the miners say the history of Nevada is mining.

The next morning after breakfast a telephone call came from the office of the governor of Nevada. His secretary introduced herself and said that our governor had viewed the *CBS Evening News* and was disturbed. "He believes that a man's home is his castle." Within the week our governor's chief of staff was walking the streets of Tuscarora, knocking on doors and hearing from voters.

Afterward he telephoned the president of Horizon at his office in Colorado. I don't know what transpired, but Horizon soon issued a press release with the promise to "preserve an historic core of Tuscarora." Details never followed, and by the end of the month Horizon was off on a different tack. All the structures would be moved some miles south to new ground, a site free of underground gold and silver. Streets would be laid out in the same pattern, but on larger lots; a municipal water and sewer treatment system installed; and a combined fire station/community center built. All of this would be done at no cost to the homeowners.

Neighbors bantered around names for this settlement: Utopia-Tuscarora, New Harmony, Walden, or Bliss. We doubted the company would ever follow through with the plan. London gold price dropped to $381 per ounce, but mining continued. The pit deepened, and more curious newscasters came by to look down into it.

The West, NBC, Sacramento, California, October 1, 1989, with John Gibson

J.G. It sounds like a happy ending. Industry comes back to life in a nearly dead town, but not in the small Nevada city [sic] we're about to take you to. The rebirth of mining there could finally kill the community. That's because the company does not want to mine around the town: they want to mine through it. Tuscarora is a postcard from God's country until you listen. [Explosions are followed by the roar of heavy equipment.] What happened in Tuscarora is that its history came alive. The problem in Tuscarora is complicated by the fact that the mine wants to expand and the town is literally in the way. The town would either have to be moved or destroyed for the mine owner to get to his claim under the town.

Technically everything in Tuscarora, including the cemetery [in the background], sits on Horizon's gold claim.

Gold speaks with a loud voice in Nevada.

There is nothing sentimental about gold.

Today Show, NBC, November 14, 1989, report by Lucky Severson
[Lucky is sitting at a bar in Elko interviewing City Councilman Barbara Errecart.]

LUCKY Unfortunately they have to bulldoze and blast away twelve tons of earth for every ounce of gold. Barbara Errecart says most of the mining companies are good citizens, most but not all.

B.E. Tuscarora is the sad part. Tuscarora is the history and how it used to be, and it's being destroyed.

LUCKY [Camera pans the mine pit and then focuses on old buildings in Tuscarora.] Today in between the sounds of progress you can hear the echos of the city that was; or maybe it's only the wind whispering through Tuscarora's remains.

There are only a few people here now, and they may have to move because Horizon Mining Company wants to expand its mine. According to a one hundred-year-old mining law, Horizon Mining Company can evict long time Tuscarora residents like world renowned potter, Dennis Parks.

I was more frightened than flattered to hear my name spoken on the *Today Show* but took some comfort when I learned how uncomfortable the president of Horizon Gold Shares was becoming.

1989 *Tuscarora* video

JOHN WATSON I think Horizon has suffered the slings and arrows of criticism from a number of different quarters, and I think it might be handy to keep in mind that Horizon isn't there to inconvenience the people in Tuscarora. Horizon is there just to make a livelihood. I think people forget that a lot.

Gold's kind of an interesting business. Ah, we work very hard, and one day somebody brings you the first bar from a mine, and you look at it, and you admire it, and then it's sent off to a refinery somewhere where they purify it even further, and then the final purified product is sent across the ocean somewhere to a very fastidious Swiss banker who looks at it, admires it, and carries it downstairs and puts it in a vault, and after all is said and done you have taken it out of the ground so he can put it back in the ground. An interesting business.

I like what I'm doing. It's my livelihood. It's my way of life: just like Dennis is an artist, I'm an entrepreneur.

Again I was not flattered. I learned how closely vanity is linked to context.

1990: During the dog days of that summer, the loud truck noises stopped, replaced by the low hum of gossip and rumor. What was Horizon up to? From across the valley a telephone call came from Linda, the schoolmarm. "Julie, aren't you guys popping champagne corks? Don't you know the mine is closing down?" A child had told her that all employees were being laid off. Horizon Gold Shares was ceasing production and would be shutting down the mine, at least temporarily.

The price of gold in London dropped to $376 per ounce. Tuscarora was quiet. Residents postponed any celebrations until the heavy equipment could be seen loaded onto flatbed trucks heading down the road out of town.

The clinking of wine glasses took place three years later, in January 1993; the party was brief, and lights in windows throughout town were off by the usual 8 P.M.

to make an end is to make a beginning / The end is where we start from.
—T. S. ELLIOT, *Four Quartets*

After power was cut to the buried pumps, the lake filled slowly: underground springs needed to be fed by the snowmelt of two winters to raise the water to the level of the bank. "Lake Lost Horizon," as it is now referred to, is larger and deeper than Pecos had promised six years earlier. I couldn't object.

Minimal reclamation of the periphery was required by both federal and state law. Horizon left a skeleton crew in charge. They continued to spray their diluted mixture of cyanide and water over the heaps of rock but added no more cyanide as sunlight gradually degraded the chemical residue. Potential deadliness dissipated until what remained was a harmless, mild, liquid fertilizer.

Swimmers with clogs and towels soon appeared on the shores of Lake Lost Horizon: to the south was a family beach and at the west a bathing-suits-optional area. Both beaches lack sand and probably will draw no tourists.

Nevada Fish and Game offered to stock the water with either black bass or rainbow trout, but Horizon's management refused, citing liability for creating an attractive nuisance. Townsfolk weren't surprised at the company's final meanspiritedness. Most residents agreed on clandestinely stocking Lake Lost Horizon, but with what species? I spoke up for sturgeon, monster fish whose presence would feed legend. Also I had read that females could be captured, milked for caviar, and then released. Julie favored pan-sized crappie; De voted for kokanee salmon; Jerry wanted catfish; and next-door neighbor Leonard, who had recently sworn off alcohol, was against all fish. "They'll only attract outsiders who'll litter the shore with beer cans." The town was back to normal with all the frogs jumping out of the wheelbarrow.

Milt, a quiet retired bookie from San Francisco, was the closest neighbor to the lake. He acted unilaterally. From an unnamed reservoir, he illegally netted fifty bass fingerlings and introduced them to the depths of Lost Horizon. After revealing his secret, he asked, "Wanta bet my bass won't be a winner in the lake?" The question of fish species had been settled.

Rough low hills surrounding the lake were an inevitable by-product

Pottery school students in front of the Tuscarora Tavern. Dennis Parks is standing, fourth from left.

of a pit being dug, and unfortunately they shall never be grass covered, as Fischer-Watt's president had promised. Jim Bob, the last Horizon employee, scattered hundreds of pounds of native grass seed, but no matter how regularly he turned on sprinklers, only a few seeds took root and sprouted in the crannies between pebbles, cobbles, and boulders. But this was enough for Jim. He bought Nona's house and retired on the corner of Weed and Main.

The lake is now a deep blue-green, the water unpolluted, and the mining speculators gone. Perhaps the residents have more character for suffering through this revival: Western philosophy seldom recommends blissfulness as a character builder. Life on the mountainside has reverted to a glacial quiet interrupted only occasionally by the shouts from neighborhood squabbles: "Was that your tomcat pissed in my pickup?" "Whose hound dog went an' killed my favorite Guinea hen?" And, of course, the fence line feuds resumed.

Rather than resurvey Tuscarora, the Elko county commissioner voted to accept a rough tax assessor map as the official plat map. Our attorney petitioned the district court and secured legal titles for the homeowners, but unfortunately some boundary descriptions don't fit neatly onto the map. The next generation can settle this.

■ Freshman Geography 101 introduced me to the subject of land and minerals. There was a poetic line in the geology textbook giving a scale of particle size: "Clay, silt, sand, pebbles, cobbles, boulders." I recall no other facts from the course, but after college, when I became serious about discovering clay, I revisited the text. In the margin next to the underlining I had added my literary addendum, "All resolves in stone or clay or poem / all that scrawling in space / the constant war / between trees and sky / on stone / tides shatter into lace."

When an English major turns into a potter, earth materials become characters central to a plot. This career shift was smooth—a bit like trading in crossword puzzles for Play-Doh. My early exploration of the Tuscarora landscape was largely motivated by thrift: no need to purchase clay and pay teamsters to deliver; I could walk around on the cheap with a shovel and gunnysack. When challenged about how much time scavenging on foot took away from my creativity in the studio, I spoke of unique geographic specificity, exercise, The Big Sky . . . until the questioner would walk away.

I thought of myself as a recycler rather than a miner: I was gleaning from the detritus of nineteenth-century underground mining. Those early workers made my labors easier because in their processes of separating out silver and gold, they also separated clay from silt and sand. This clay was not very plastic, but bountiful: a free supply of native earthenware that fired to a healthy burnt orange in the kiln.

Dig-your-own-clay added a pedagogical value for students who were accustomed to finding only gray clay premixed in clear plastic sacks. The unavoidable twigs and leaves that came with Tuscarora clay we simply scooped off the top of the water while the dry material soaked in a washtub. Next I instructed students to pour the clay slurry into shallow trenches, which we had dug and lined with old bed sheets. Within several hours the dry earth sucked out excess moisture, leaving clay that was ready to use. The raw yellowish-brown color and mushy texture challenged the squeamish. Not all students enjoyed this experience, but education is often that way.

Besides this particular clay, other promising deposits were discovered, processed, fired, and evaluated. West of town lay a massive, white tailing pile resting on a small hill beside a mine shaft. From a distance this pale blur, so out of place in the sagebrush, resembled a beached dead whale. Undergraduates dug Moby Dick clay enthusiastically but were subsequently disheartened by the results. The clay included minute limestone particles, which would pop out after firing, leaving distinct, unaesthetic, acne-like scars.

At the conclusion of a fishing trip I was on my knees by the bank of the Owyhee, pulling up watercress for garnish, when I noticed a gray clay clinging to roots. Some days later I returned with student labor. For me this was a joy—standing in the shallows with pant legs rolled up over my knees. I could pause from my digging and watch brook trout dash off and crayfish scurry backward. This was not comforting to my barefoot students.

The wet clay was smooth between my toes and later in the studio between my fingers. Companions were youngsters who had been reared in suburbia; from experience they rightfully believed that bodies of water should rest on either a firm foundation of concrete or silky beach sand.

Novices are seldom drawn to study clay by the mysteries of its origin or the demanding processes involved in transforming mud into art. Students yearn for finished products. One fall a rank beginner arrived with a Christmas list: names of friends and relatives followed by rough sketches of objects envisioned under a tree.

During our forays I overheard whispered complaints, but organized insurrection never formed. During the heady days of the 1960s, this was tacit approval of a teacher's performance.

Riverbed clay failed: the clay deformed into a dark brown lava before the glaze on its surface had melted. I knew that chemically clay and glaze were quite similar, but to transform the former into the latter usually a few grams of this or that flux was needed. Students referred to our spectacular learning experience as the latest disaster, and they reverted to using the reliable old Tuscarora red.

"Success can only lead to repetition and self-plagiarism" were my parting words as I left the studio and walked to my study. Alone, without disciples, I plotted a strategy: order assorted high-temperature clays, which I could blend into a stoneware body; then I could experiment applying riverbed clay for glaze. I purchased dry materials: fire clay from California, ball clay from Kentucky, and feldspar from Arizona.

At this juncture, as I was going commercial, I still continued exploring for local materials, but now testing them for their utility as glazes. Initially the fired results produced varying hues of brown, some glossy, some matte. My favorite was concocted with mud chips—those thin, curly flakes that form on the surface of dry potholes in dirt roads. The resulting glaze would have been admired as Temoku by Japanese connoisseurs: a glossy brown with a smattering of fascinating black and rust-red spots. American tourists, on the contrary, asked if I didn't by chance have some blue pots in a back room.

Customers also wanted greens, yellows, and reds. Occasionally, visit-

Students Sana Musasama and Michelle McCurdy firing the kiln.

Parks and student Lisa Neave inspecting pottery.

ing potters complimented me on my subtle earth colors, but they never bought a piece. I ordered a few pounds of cobalt from Zaire and red iron oxide from Spain to brighten up my palette.

Historically, the first evidence of glaze on stoneware comes from China during the Shang Dynasty around 1500 B.C. When flames waffled through their kilns, wood ash was deposited on lips and shoulders of vessels and later melted into a runny granular glaze. By happenstance Chinese potters progressed to sifting dry wood ash, which was mixed in water with powdered clay and then applied prior to firing.

Ash from burned vegetation contains varying quantities of the essentials: silica, alumina, and flux. Percentages are determined by the plant species and the composition of the earth where a plant grows. Roots function as conduits for both water and minerals. I've overheard exploration geologists speak of burning plants from a particular locale in order to analyze the ash for evidence of mining potential.

Close beside the old mill sites on the outskirts of Tuscarora are weathered heaps of sagebrush ash. These bushes grew from three to seven feet tall and provided the only fuel available to power the nineteenth-century Tuscarora steam engines.

When sagebrush ash is sifted through a fine screen onto the top of a stoneware vessel, then fired to 2,400 °F, the fine dust melts and matures as a glossy, smooth, utilitarian glaze. The browns are muted, merely background for those sought-after highlights of blue, green, and yellow, which sparkle.

After these pleasing results were unloaded from a kiln, my students were more attentive and soon switched from earthenware to stoneware generously dusted with sagebrush ash. Often I left them to rummage alone for other discarded materials. Coffee cans in the glaze room filled with broken bits of glass, square nails, rock samples, and other detritus. Former students and potters who had passed through sent back exotic ashes from around the country: mountain mahogany from the Ruby Mountains, mixed hardwood from the Midwest, volcanic dust from Mount Saint Helens, eucalyptus and lemonwood from the West Coast, and aspen from Aspen.

This search for the unusual led me to make an inquiry with Jack, the FBI agent from Elko. He was only a sporadic customer but regularly dropped in to seek my help locating this or that character on a wanted poster. Deep rural does offer cover where an escapee or parole violator can easily disguise himself with a cowboy hat pulled low. I was never able to help with an arrest, but this didn't stop me from asking a favor in return. An item on the TV morning news had piqued my interest about how tons of marijuana confiscated all over the West Coast was regularly incinerated at a central facility in the San Francisco area. I figured it wouldn't hurt to ask. I explained how the ash would be put to good use.

Removing freshly fired pottery from the stoneware kiln. Left to right: Julie Parks, Dennis Parks, and student Sid Di Garmo.

Kilns in the snow.

While he was mulling over my initial proposal, I asked another favor. "Jack, would it be too much trouble to request that the agents label the ash according to origin? You know, like . . . hydroponically grown in Beverly Hills, from the highlands of Central Mexico, Mendocino Coast . . . whatever." I briefly outlined how growing conditions affect mineral content.

He passed me the latest wanted poster and said, "You know, I'll check on that, Parks. I do have friends who work on that incinerator."

Evidently, rumor of my recycling circulated through Elko, because one day a craps dealer from the Stockman's Casino walked into my studio lugging a five-gallon bucket filled to the brim with a black, sandy material that he said was copper concentrate.

"You know, it's that ore they ship out of Battle Mountain. This fell by the railroad tracks where they load up."

I thanked him as I labeled the bucket and placed it on a shelf between coconut ash and cow dung ash.

"You know, if it works in your kiln, I can get you more. It's just lying all around . . . free for the taking."

I thanked him again. This was a bonanza. Copper is the mineral necessary to produce red glazes and, when purchased from a catalog, one of the most expensive.

"Glad I can help," he said as we shook hands and parted. "Let me know how it comes out. I thought you'd like this stuff because . . . well . . . because people said that you use weird, local shit in your glazes."

CHAPTER **5**

The Long Bumpy Road

Between January and April the last seven miles to Tuscarora are covered in mud or snow, which discourages visitors. Only Saint Bette, the contract mail carrier, drives in regularly—8 A.M. Monday through Saturday. For twenty years, Sharon-the-Postmaster sorted the incoming mail into individual boxes or into canvas sacks for the ranches: Taylor Canyon, Van Norman, Wright, Spanish, Mori, Jack Creek, Deep Creek, I.L., and Petan.

By 9 A.M. Saint Bette has loaded the ranch mail back into her pickup, referred to as "the Stage," and she begins a fifty-mile drive north. Her title was bestowed after many kindnesses beyond duty: delivering forgotten necessities from Elko, such as a grocery item, a prescription, an emergency bouquet.

Bette is back at noon to deliver mail from the ranches and pick up Tuscarora's outgoing mail. In the meantime the Postmaster has opened the counter for the sale of stamps and money orders. Residents drift in to check their boxes, exchange gossip and weather predictions, and perhaps check out a book or audio tape. The lobby doubles as a branch of the county library. Contemporary rural life had acquired amenities. Every home is connected to electric power and telephone service; four have computers, and one a fax machine. Sports fans install satellite dishes; the rest of us rely on rabbit ears for morning news and weather.

From May through December an unaccountable number of strangers drive up the road, slowly circling the streets and stopping here or there to roll down the window and capture a snapshot. Because pottery is the only business in town, and Americans love to shop when they travel, sooner or later the cars park in front of the hotel. The door remains unlocked, and lights are bright in the hallway. In the front door window, under the plastic OPEN sign, is a note for visitors who wish to be shown around—walk out back to the studios; or when no one is working, an alternate note directs potential customers up Main Street to our house. Usually these instructions are preempted because one of us has seen or heard the car.

I was interviewed by an author researching a book on the twentieth-century frontier. In the nineteenth century our government classified Western lands as frontier when the average population was one resident or fewer per square mile; with this definition, Elko County still qualified. Driving north from the county seat of Elko (population 25,000) toward Idaho, a car could pass through Tuscarora (12), Mountain City (30), and Owyhee (400) with mostly sagebrush in between. Cartographers mark all these population clusters. Some maps even include deserted mining camps like Cornucopia and Blue Jacket, where no buildings exist and the vestigial roads would challenge the bravest of SUV drivers.

Authors of travel guides seem equally desperate for material. All the books describing Nevada include a paragraph or two directing travelers to the town of Tuscarora. Writers may visit to interview locals and take photographs; but occasionally the Postmaster receives inquiries, which she puts in my box.

Unexpectedly a TV crew might arrive and spend half a day filming local color and decaying buildings; a newscaster with his microphone asks questions like, "Why do you live in Tuscarora?" "Were you born here?" And every few years a young newspaper reporter drops by the studio for a morsel of rural human interest. The questions are similar.

Summer brings migrating ceramic artists, professors, and students on the horizon. Some student types arrive to work in the studios; others just drop in to see what's happening. With the casual, after I answer some questions about clay, glazes, and firing, I suggest we all go fishing. Walking rapidly downstream at this altitude limits conversation and puts color into pale, young cheeks. Older guests often prefer to sit out on the lawn in the shade sipping beverages. Gossip from the outside world is delightful, in moderation. In the warm months I get very little work done in my studio. If I make a sale to one of these guests, it is an unexpected by-product.

■ Ceramists often know where I live because I wrote a manuscript "Glazed Raw & Fired Free," which was subsequently published (*A Potter's Guide to Raw Glazing and Oil Firing*, New York: Charles Scribner's Sons; London: Pitman). The text concentrated on the timesaving techniques of applying glaze to raw, dry clay and firing a single time in a kiln fueled with waste automotive oil. Unfamiliar techniques to most, but efficiency and recycling were popular themes. More people came to visit me, and wide distribution of the text led to invitations for me to travel and speak.

After a conference in St. Louis, Missouri, where I was on a panel discussing alternative fuels, a young man introduced himself by saying he had enjoyed and profited from reading the book. He explained how he had partially followed my instructions and how he had deviated. His studio was nestled in the center of a suburban neighborhood, and he feared that those close by would not long tolerate the odor of crankcase oil burning (that familiar, but concentrated, smell of a freeway at rush hour). He opted for a more pleasant odor, associated with the lobby of fast-food restaurants. He fabricated the burners for his kiln according to diagrams in my book: the fuel he recycled was old french fry oil from

Dennis Parks unloading a kiln. Photo by Julie Parks.

the burger joint where he worked part-time. He successfully fired a kiln to 2,400 °F with suburban-friendly smells. When he ran low on this fuel he made acquaintance with employees at a nearby donut franchise who were happy to get rid of their rancid vegetable oil in exchange for an occasional handmade coffee mug. Neighbors, next door to the kiln, thought this innovation the finest. I do not remember his name, but donuts make me think of him. They make me optimistic.

■ Potential buyers can be intuited on sight because they do not arrive in period VW buses or on motorcycles. Also sales are rarely made to graying owners of motor homes or tobacco-chewing cowboys in pickup trucks hauling a horse trailer. For some years I also predicted the likelihood of a sale by the color of the arriving car. I discovered empirically, with no aesthetic or psychological underpinnings, that drivers of red cars were the most likely. Unfortunately, today touring the Western states is most often done in a rental; the driver has little or no choice of model or color. Travelers fly into Salt Lake City or Reno, sign up for a car, and purchase a guidebook.

Currently, the probability of a sale is gauged by the proximity of a parked car to my front gate. If the driver has stopped on our side of Main Street, close to the gate, prospects are good. If the car rests on the far side, but opposite the gate, the probability is strong. But any driver who parks two or more car-lengths away only wants to ask questions about my life in Tuscarora.

The historian Arthur Schlesinger says questions that no one has a right to ask are not entitled to a truthful answer. I agree with him if awkward questions come at me in a crowded cocktail party, but out here sophistication mellows and the threshold is lower for both asking and answering intrusive questions. My Tuscarora answers may be a simple yes or no, or a grunt, and Julie says that sometimes I give a flippant reply. But in all instances I am attempting to be honest.

Visitors usually pop questions after I have given them a free docent tour of the showroom up front and then guided them out back through the studios and around the kiln yard. We return to the front of the hotel by way of the long lawn I manicure on the north side. Mowing, fertilizing, and watering are justified on the theory that the bright green landscape distracts from the run-down wood exterior of the building. Visitors meander slowly among pedestaled sculptures on the path shaded by a mature apple tree. Questions begin:

1. "Why do you live so far away?"
2. "Were you born here?"
3. "You must like it?"
4. "Have you ever been to Pittsburgh?"
5. "Don't you ever get bored?"

"No," I answered to the last question. I have thought of elaborating with a string of my own questions: How could I get bored when I have no proper job? How could I get bored working in the studio making whatever whenever I please? I can stretch out on my sofa by a wood stove and read the weekly *New Yorker* from cover to cover before the next issue arrives, or explore above town looking for the makings of a salad, or spend my day with a fishing rod. How could I be bored when each day is filled with all those activities a regularly employed worker dreams of indulging in after sixty-five?

Only once when I was very impatient I answered, "Hey, if I want to get bored, I can buy myself a TV satellite dish." The visitor beamed and replied, "Really, so you can have entertainment up here. That's good." This encouraged me to revert to short answers.

■ A middle-aged woman drove up in a dark green convertible and parked on the wrong side of Main Street. I walked slowly up from the studio and across the lawn, all the while patting my trouser legs to clean off the clay dust. She kept her distance as I introduced myself and opened the front door. She appeared overdressed for shopping in Tusca-

Dennis Parks at the potter's wheel. Photo by Valerie Parks.

rora, but once she was in the showroom all her pastel colors glowed against the background of earth-colored glazes. Her orange lipstick was remarkable because it had been applied broadly with little relationship to the perimeter of her lips. Her perfume lingered, but I remembered her more for her parting question. She had walked a slow circle in the center of the room, never lifting or touching a pot. On exiting, she paused and we stood face to face when she asked, "Why does all pottery look like some Indian made it?"

▨ Julie told me of showing a particularly thoughtful young woman around Tuscarora. The visitor had purchased some pottery and then asked if it were possible to have a guided tour of town. Julie, by nature accommodating, took the lead down to the remains of Chinatown, over the old schoolhouse, pointed out the Masonic Lodge and the only brick home, down at the west end of Weed Street. Julie said this woman was unusually quiet and nodded at the end of Julie's narratives. Finally, the visitor spoke, "You know, it's funny. The only noise I hear in this town is the sound of our footsteps. Does that ever spook you?" Julie paused, and the woman continued, "Oh, of course it doesn't bother you. That's probably why you live here."

■ "Can you really make a living?" I nod. My father refused to answer any questions about how much money he made. After he accepted a position as historian at the Department of State and we moved from Berea, Kentucky, to Washington, D.C., he did confide, to the family, that his salary had doubled. That was as detailed as he would be. He could ramble on and on with minutia about the federal budget, the cost of the Panama Canal, and the New Deal (with special emphasis on the benefits of the TVA) but was quiet if I asked how much our house cost.

Naturally, I am taken aback when an outsider asks about my financial health. "You and your wife really afford to live year 'round here?" "And you raised children out here?" I speculate that there is some effect on seemingly decent tourists, perhaps the Big Sky and the quiet, that turns them into Peeping Toms.

I have thought to myself and spoken with Julie about what would constitute a complete and honest explanation. With close urban friends, who are too polite to ask, I still sense the submerged question: "How the hell do Parkses survive?" Rurals can appear aberrant to urban couples who are both employed at serious jobs with regular paychecks and have never doubted the prevailing American ethos that financial security buffered with weekends of popular entertainment is the basis of a normal, well-rounded life. Our old friends seem tolerant of others who have chosen a different road to travel, but on occasion I catch a hint that they detect an underlying recklessness, mild irresponsibility, and a possible

Julie Parks's hotel kitchen. Photo by Ron Moroni.

self-indulgence. Other friends who aspire to personal goals less eco-
nomic than most, but more spiritual than mine, refer to our family life
in Tuscarora as being blessed. Both camps agree that those Parkses
stumbled onto a lot of good luck.

Truth is we have survived from the sale of pottery and Julie's part-
time employment at the post office and aided by summer student fees,
which were not sufficient for salary but supported a year-round studio.
Our combined income was probably never greater than that of a beginning public school teacher in Mississippi.

While residing in California, spectacular, financial good fortune was
dealt us, but I didn't realize what we were holding until years later in
Nevada when we cashed in.

A neighboring college in Claremont was preparing to level an old
office building and clear the area for a new parking lot. Cabinets, tables,
chairs, and files had to be moved to other buildings, but apparently the

The Plunkett house after remodeling. This is now the residence of Dennis and Julie Parks.

administration lacked space to house all the furniture. Their faculty had been invited in to pick and choose. Still, many useful items remained unclaimed. On the last day before demolition, faculty from nearby colleges were alerted.

I arrived at four in the afternoon with my pickup truck and parked between two bulldozers. A custodian pointed me in the direction and asked if I would please hurry. I shuffled through dust and debris, past a pile of chairs with missing legs, rolls of frayed throw rugs, a line of chipped Formica tables, and suddenly I saw an object I'd never seen before—an octagonal-shaped dark wood table. The surface was deeply scratched and appeared to have been a home for ancient worms. Though the legs were crudely carved, they curved gracefully and definitely embodied ornamental intent.

The table was approximately five feet in diameter and conveniently constructed in two halves. Alone I was able to manage loading the sections onto the bed of my truck.

Because we had been residing in Claremont for only two months, our living room was open to decorating. I arranged the halves flush on opposing walls, facing each other. Before Julie returned from work, I had dusted and oiled my acquisition. Because all of our other furniture was used, worn, and abused, this table did not stand out.

Julie commented that it was certainly centuries older than anything from Salvation Army and perhaps in my free time after classes I could fix it up. I looked at the table and thought that someday I should sand down the top, fill all the worm holes with plastic wood, and paint on a couple of coats of Varathane. I never did, and my procrastination preserved our windfall.

For the next four years in California and twenty-two in Nevada, the only attention this table received was a regular dusting and the occasional squirt of Lemon Pledge. It was the centerpiece in the hotel in our display room; the surface was hidden under an embroidered tablecloth trimmed in lace, which covered the rough edges. The aroma of Pledge helped more with sales than the presence of the antique. Visitors remarked on the age of the exposed legs as they might after coming upon a derelict outdoor privies, "That's certainly interesting wood." I learned to love the old octagon: I worried about fire, but never theft.

James, a student from Long Island with a background in art history and interior design, believed not only that this table was very old but also that it might be very valuable. At that time, Parks's finances were low but not bottomed out. I had no desire to part with the piece prematurely. If it was truly a priceless antique, it would only grow older.

Before James moved on to San Francisco, I photographed the table and gave him a set of prints. Within a month he wrote back that he had shown these to a dealer who made an offer on the spot. James advised not to sell. I should receive more at an auction.

The offer he passed on was tempting: enough to purchase a good, used, two-wheel-drive pickup. I sensed that this was not enough. I would miss the table. James suggested that I mail a packet of photos to Christie's art auction house in New York City.

The table was trucked to San Francisco for inclusion with a larger shipment of other Western treasures bound for Christie's. The auction house had written, estimating that my table should sell in the mid-thousands, more than twice the San Francisco dealer's offer. Months passed before I received another letter from Christie's. Enclosed was a bill in the high hundreds for the cost of crating and shipping the table and a smaller bill for catalog photography. At the bottom of the page, in small print, was a statement of company policy whereby in the case an item does not sell the owner will be billed daily for storage. The auction process was looking less like entering a sweepstakes and more like feeding dollars into a slot machine.

The telephone rang at 9 A.M. in Tuscarora, noon in New York City. A female voice introduced herself as an agent at Christie's, and in an excited voice said, "I didn't want you to have to wait any longer. Last night your Italian Renaissance walnut octagonal center table, number 127, sold for over three times our estimate." We had made a killing. Even after subtracting expenses and commission, the check would be enough to purchase a new, four-wheel-drive diesel pickup truck with all the extras—had we been in need of one. The old Land Rover was still running.

Instead we called Colorado for our old friend, John the carpenter, who drove north with his tools. Julie's kitchen was upgraded a full century: contemporary appliances, refrigerator recessed into the wall, Formica counters with walls and ceiling painted to match, and cabinets with hinged doors. John cut a large opening in the ceiling of the hotel showroom and installed a skylight. Sunlight shone down on the spot where the table had stood. He installed track lighting and paneled the hallway in wainscot. A smell of fresh paint came into our lives. The remaining cash from our windfall dribbled off here and there.

■ I have no memory of my father speaking of luck. Elijah Taylor Parks was born in 1898 on a rocky farm in central Tennessee, the eldest son among seven children. He worked his way through college to a Ph.D.; and even though he graduated into the Great Depression, from his subsequent teaching salary he sent money home to help three siblings graduate from college. Dad died in Washington, D.C., in June 1966, a month before the Tuscarora Pottery School opened. Had he lived longer, he would have been uncomfortable visiting here; and although he wouldn't have mentioned it, he certainly would have been in agreement with our friends who doubted the practicality of a rural quest.

My father told stories of a young man plowing cornfields for fifty cents a day and peddling eggs for a nickel a dozen, later losing his small savings in a bank closure and watching long lines of the unemployed waiting at soup kitchens. I was fascinated listening, but I never could identify with the plot. These were tales from a world I knew nothing about. I grew up in the post–World War II prosperity: my only experience with banks was the tellers who handed out lollipops; newspapers reported a man who attempted to starve himself to death being taken to the hospital and force fed with tubes; even the slow-witted and unambitious of my college contemporaries were hired into responsible, well-paying jobs.

■ Julie and I married in North Carolina. Together we packed a VW bus for travel. For security she held a B.S. in nursing from Duke University, and I carried a B.A. in English literature from the University of North Carolina. The trek led us to Iowa; then back east to Washington, D.C., where Ben and Greg were born, before we headed west to northern California; down to Los Angeles, where I added an M.F.A. degree; off to Illinois; back to Southern California; and finally to rest in Tuscarora. An adventure. Not motivated by rebellion, just curiosity. Employment was peripheral: a mix of part time and full time. We suppressed desires for possessions without experiencing any deprivation. Whatever didn't fit in a VW bus was left behind.

Even the IRS could not destroy my feeling that our young family was doing just fine. During the Nixon era the government classified our income below the poverty line, and for two years in a row we received unrequested, supplementary income checks. The amount would not have saved the truly poor from hunger, but we were joyous for a little extra. Poverty is a relative term; we never felt poor.

▒ In 1999, on the morning news, I watched Roberto Benigni receive his Oscar for best actor. He hopped up the steps like a frog, grasped the microphone, smiled at the camera, and in heavily accented English thanked his parents in Italy, "For poverty." Perhaps I misunderstood, but anyway I hoped Ben and Greg were watching.

▒ From my freshman year in college I have only one friend I keep in touch with. He was called Snake, the perfect nickname for a student studying to become an attorney. Today he has a successful criminal defense practice in the San Francisco area. I visited him regularly when our sons were in college. The subject of poverty came up once when I was helping him move into a small apartment after his second divorce. "You would have split up too . . . like everyone else of our generation. It's normal today. But you and Julie . . . you two never had enough of anything to divide in half."

A rural setting doesn't encourage splitting up. During the growing season it would be untimely to separate; not after you worked hard together in the vegetable garden, digging, planting seeds, watering, and hoeing weeds; certainly not before the final harvest as winter sets in. And then with snow blanketing the town, a couple is drawn closer together. Even dogs don't want to leave our bed to sniff out adventure. The next time I visited Snake I argued against the poverty theory: the secret is horticulture and body heat. Of course this combination might prove invalid in a centrally heated apartment building, crowded into a landlocked neighborhood.

Dennis and Julie Parks on the porch of the Plunkett house, with their American pit bull terriers. Photo by Gary Nichaman.

Our level of relative poverty probably did contribute to Ben and Greg growing up resourceful and independent. At the beginning of our first winter in the mountains, they disparaged the perfectly good, clean, warm coats Julie had picked out in a thrift store. The boys circled goose down arctic jackets in an REI catalog and would buy them with their own money, which they planned to earn after school by trapping muskrats in the Owyhee River. I had no experience that would help them in this enterprise.

Our neighbor, Butters, invited them across the street to a shed behind his house where he gave them a dozen small, vicious, steel-jawed traps and an introductory lecture on how to set them in action. Randy, the schoolmarm's husband, had given up on small animals in favor of coyotes and bobcats, and contributed additional small traps and also led the boys on a field trip down along the river, instructing them on subtleties.

Ben and Greg were in the independent fur business. The first Euro-Americans who explored northeastern Nevada were doing the same, but on horseback. Ben drove a Land Rover, and Greg, with legs too short, but wearing the longer irrigator boots, was responsible for wading into the water when emergencies arose.

They targeted muskrats, though occasionally a mink was bagged, and only once they intentionally trapped a beaver, which proved very tiresome to skin. Then by mistake they caught one mean river otter. Standard bait was a slice of apple, enhanced with drops of anise oil, impaled on a willow stick, which was stuck into the shoreline and overhung shallow water.

The little dead animals were skinned in our backyard and the pelts stretched on boards like inside-out stockings. Remaining fat was scraped from the skin, and then these hides were propped inside a shed to dry for several days before being stuffed into a gunny sack and mailed to a buyer in Salt Lake City. By late winter, Ben and Greg were wearing down-filled coats.

The fateful afternoon when they trapped the otter turned into

Ben and Greg Parks working with their muskrat traps. The boys sold the pelts to earn spending money. Photos by Julie Parks.

evening before I heard the Land Rover park outside our house. My worries had changed to annoyance by the time they walked into the house, but before I could say anything they were standing in front of me with big smiles. "Look at this," they said in unison. Ben was holding a dead otter by the tail, an animal I had seen only pictured in the children's book, *Ring of Bright Water*, when the boys were smaller and their hands cleaner.

Both boys, interrupting and correcting each other, told a story of the hissing, angry, toothy otter who after stepping into the trap had done all he could to escape. The wire anchoring the trap to shore was torn free, and the otter swam to the opposite side only to get this trailing wire entangled in low willow branches where the boys spied him. Ben sent little Greg with the tall boots into the stream with a big stick to dispatch and retrieve.

Occasionally I would accompany them for an afternoon walk along the riverbank as they collected their bounty and reset traps. I watched Greg pull a trap out of the water which had by happenstance snapped shut on the tail of a small brook trout. The boys laughed and then Greg smashed the fish dead on a rock. Next he replaced the apple bait with an impaled fish. "Dad, you'll see . . . tomorrow I'll have a mink here."

The next day, sure enough, when they came home, in their sack of muskrats was one long mink. "I told you so, Dad," Greg said as they began the task of skinning. I stood around, curious to see them loosen pelts with a new technique they had just learned from a friend at school. Instead of laboriously separating fur from meat with sharp knives, Ben made just a small incision on a back leg and inserted a sports needle, the common variety used to inflate playground balls. A bicycle pump was activated, and the animal quickly swelled up double in size. Once deflated, with the pelt loosened from the flesh, only a minimum of cutting and scraping finished the job. A father raised in suburbia was astonished.

Gory outdoorsy stories were seldom retold for the amusement of tourists who asked if my children weren't bored living here. Instead, I would detail how interesting the rural education system is, and how different from the American norm. I could point across the valley at a speck just at the base of the Independence Mountain Range.

Up close the school is a cement block rectangle divided into two rooms. On average there are ten to sixteen students enrolled in grades one through eight instructed by a single schoolmarm. Parents are responsible for transporting their children. Most commute from ranches more remote than Tuscarora, so a snowstorm was an unacceptable excuse for the boys being absent or tardy.

When I visited the school grounds I witnessed none of the vicious age and sex discrimination that I remember participating in when growing up. The enrollment is so minuscule that when organizing softball or basketball games, every little body, no matter how undeveloped, was drafted. Here it was normal to watch a sixth-grade boy gently coach and encourage a first-grade girl. These games were rough and played with the usual shouting and screaming, but with a surprising lack of interest in a final score.

Hard-nosed competition was reserved for indoors, the academic arena. There was always at least one other student at both Ben and Greg's grade level—an opponent to be watched closely and never allowed to race ahead in the assignment book or to score higher on a test. Skipping a day of school to go fishing with Dad would have been like having the coach bench you in a championship series.

Because the Elko County school board was distant, the administrators kept track of rural students' progress by scrutinizing the results of regular standardized tests. At first I doubted the pedagogical value of this system, but as the boys progressed and succeeded in high school and later college, I concluded that a student's confidence and experience with true-false and multiple-choice tests is an educational asset to be valued right up there with knowledge.

Younger students at the Independence Valley School were never viewed as competitors by the older ones. The teacher encouraged those

Ben Parks and Davey Logan with homemade "armor." Growing up in Tuscarora encouraged strong traits of self-sufficiency and creativity. Photo by Larry and Joan Logan.

in the higher grades, when they had finished their own assignments, to move their desks over and tutor. Of course, this practice benefited older and younger alike and allowed the teacher extra time with first graders.

After Ben graduated from the eighth grade, he boarded with an older couple in Elko, the standard practice with ranch families. But the following year when Greg was ready to enter high school, my mother proposed buying a house in the city. She had started auditing evening classes at the community college and didn't relish the long drives home after dark. She and Julie went shopping for real estate and found a small, three-bedroom house a block from the high school and less than a mile from the college.

Julie and I covered house payments until both boys graduated. The women worked out a schedule so that one was always in town. I tried to step up pottery production to cover expenses, but every Wednesday I scheduled a break to drive in to Elko by way of a pizza parlor and host lunch. The boys retreated to Tuscarora on weekends except during basketball season.

Their academic combativeness intensified in high school and led naturally to high grades and early talk of which elite distant college they would apply to. They didn't consider community college real.

Family income stalled at the high end of poverty. I figured that the time had arrived when I should consider returning to serious teaching, somewhere where faculty children were not billed. My curriculum vitae was a thicket of exhibitions, museum acquisitions, awards, honors, and a bibliography of articles written by and about. I went ahead and signed a contract with Charles Scribner & Sons to write a text on ceramic techniques.

Visiting professors went uncharacteristically quiet when I laid out my plan. One alluded to a decade of changes in academia where CV's were still important, of course, but ethnicity and gender were now factored in . . . i.e., forget it, Parks.

Fortunately, a career change was not in order. The boys said they didn't want it. When they filled out college statements on family finance, admission departments replied that this income was low enough that, together with high grades, such candidates qualified for generous scholarships. I was delighted when both my sons were eligible, and I boasted of these awards to a middle-class academic friend who countered by saying that on campus such financial aid packages were referred to as "poor-white-trash scholarships." Ben and Greg laughed.

Before the boys moved to Elko for high school, they had pulled their muskrat traps, hung them in a shed, and henceforth earned extra money with a string of summer jobs. While still in elementary school they had experience working on a ranch moving and connecting irrigation pipes. After they reached the legal age for employment they were hired sequentially by the state highway maintenance crew to flag cars. While Ben worked his summer on the roads, Greg signed up as a cowboy. Later he tallied his paychecks, subtracting expenses for leather saddle, silver spurs, high-crowned cowboy hat, and warm bedroll. Then he said, "Dad, I think I'll study to be a veterinarian. Maybe I could buy a ranch and hire the cowboys." Ben expressed career plans only much later.

Their summer employment that paid the best came with the boom in exploration for microscopic gold across the valley. Strong young men could find long hours and good pay in dirty, exhausting labor as drill helpers. The college library was very attractive to return to in the fall. I have recommended these jobs to urban fathers with truculent children who contemplate dropping out of school.

■ Jiří, a Central European artist, was visiting the United States for the first time. He said, "Thank you, may I ask how much welcome did neighbors give you and Julie when you were strangers?" He was seated at the head of the dining room table, leafing through a box of old black-and-white photographs that recorded our early years in Tuscarora and scrutinizing a particular snapshot that had captured us standing in front of the tavern. "You and Julie look much like hippies!"

Those rumors I had always countered by reciting a litany of our middle-classness: two houses, two cars, one marriage, two children, three dogs, a cat, a hamster, and an excess of college degrees. For Jiří this did not explain the details of the yellowing photograph, which was a close-up of a male in his thirties with a freshly shaved head and sporting a full, unkempt beard. Julie was beside me, a smiling, vivacious woman with long, straight, blonde hair wearing a patchwork vest that was held together with bright chrome studs and, as I remember, had embroidered on the back "Mother Trucker." Also the angle of the composition was misleading. A bolt on the metal door behind my left ear appeared to be an earring. Jiří asked if I had had a Harley Davidson motorcycle.

"Thank you I like hippies. Today in Prague many young people dress weird, too." I wanted to divert this line of conversation with photos of the early kilns, but before I found them he picked up another photo of the founders. Here I was posed standing beside Julie in the center of Weed Street: she wore a long denim dress and was holding a bouquet of wilted wildflowers; I was outfitted in my best marrying-and-burying garb—a double-breasted black business suit, dusty Tony Lama boots, and a wide-brimmed black cowboy hat accented with a thin silver band. The beard had been shaved, but a long, waxed mustache remained. Jiří looked up from the photo, smiled broadly, and said, "Fantashtish!"

Jiří was not alone in believing that hippies had once inhabited the area. Early one fall a car with Utah license plates drove in and parked on the wrong side of the street. I was standing out front of the hotel dressed as an ordinary potter in clay-spattered Levi's and T-shirt. I approached the car just as the driver's window rolled down. "Hello, would you like me to show you around the pottery?"

"Nope, but thanks anyway. We came up to see those hippies . . . sister-in-law in Elko told us about 'em . . . said there were at least three hundred living in some old mine shafts. Think they'd mind me taking a few flash pictures?"

I explained that presently only fifteen people lived in Tuscarora, most of these were senior citizens drawing Social Security, and all of us lived in either a house or a trailer. My family was the most youthful, but that day I probably resembled a bricklayer more than a love child. Even my long-haired summer students had left town and returned to college.

"Can't you at least show us the caves?"

I politely told the truth. All mine shafts I have located in the area are vertical, deep, and uninhabitable holes. Those nearest a road have been used for decades as garbage dumps. Even drug-addled flower children would find these cavities frightening and disgusting. Bad karma for making love and music.

Curiosity turned hostile when I corrected the wording of his next question, "Well, where is that old Chinese bridge?"

I pointed down the gully, but had to add, "The bridge is at the south end of old Chinatown, but technically it's not Chinese. It was built in 1969 by an art student from California." Had this young bridge builder still been in the area he would have satisfied their urge for a photograph: six-foot-eight with shoulder-length hair and a scraggly beard and a chipmunk grin.

A voice from the backseat of the car piped out as the driver's window was rolling up, "Why don't you ask the gentleman where those marijuana fields are. Sally said the hippies had over three thousand acres." The car drove off, and I waved.

Hippie sleuths would have liked my mother's stories of her youth, though I doubt she would have allowed a photograph. She insisted that recent photographs didn't look like her. She was even annoyed at her reflection in storefront windows. "They all make me look like an old woman."

She grew up in the 1920s in a restless family. I saw her as a proto- or ur-hippie. Photographed in her salad days, she was tall, statuesque, and handsome, with dark hair cascading down to her waist. A garland of wild flowers was visible around her forehead, and the glasses were identical to John Lennon's. Her father, Will, played the mandolin and she the violin; sister sang soprano; and her mother painted on Sundays.

Tuscarora's "Chinese Bridge," actually constructed in 1969 by Jay Cushman, an art/engineering under-graduate student from California.

In 1921, Will up and quit his job as an accountant for a Massachusetts paper mill, drove home, and asked the womenfolk what they would think of moving to California. They sold or discarded all possessions that wouldn't fit in or on top of their 1917 Buick sedan, leaving barely enough space for two adults, two adolescent girls, and a fox terrier.

As they drove west, toward evening they would pitch tent in a campsite or in a wide spot beside the road. My grandmother, Florence, had made bedrolls from felt blankets discarded at the paper mill. In transit they cooked over an open fire and bathed modestly in tree-lined streams.

After passing through Kansas City, the Lincoln Highway became a gravel road. From there on, streets were paved only within city limits. When they crossed the Nevada-California border and were ascending Donner Summit, first gear proved too weak for the grade. Will pulled over, turned the car around, and drove up the Sierra Nevada Range in reverse. Dependability of the brakes on the descent worried Will, so he stopped at the peak and chopped down a tree, which he chained to the rear bumper and dragged behind them until the road flattened out.

From Sacramento, Will drove south to Riverside, where a distant uncle lived. Reasons why my grandparents were still restless are lost in family history, but within months they packed up again to return to New England. The car retraced the same roads, again backwards up Donner Summit, and dragging a fresh log down the slope into Nevada.

Winter was locked into Massachusetts. Jobs were sparse, but the nomadic spirit was still bright. Someone suggested, "What about Florida?" The family drove south and passed the winter in a warm, muddy tent city located just beyond the last trolley stop outside Saint Petersburg. All four found jobs in the city; my mother and her sister did not enroll in school and instead worked at a five-and-dime. Mother confessed later that though she never heard of marijuana, she did smoke dried corn silks on the sly with new friends.

The East Coast/West Coast dilemma was settled in the spring when they packed the car and headed back to Riverside, California, returning by a flatter, southern route through New Mexico and Arizona, and settled down in a home next door to Will's distant uncle.

After graduating from high school, my mother studied poetry and geography at UCLA. When she finally joined us in Tuscarora, the lay of the land was not strange. She moved into the one-room Plunkett house and lived the first winter with neither electricity nor indoor plumbing: I installed two propane lamps and a small wood stove and built what proved to be a drafty outhouse. More sunlight came into her home through the windows than would have through the mouth of a cave, but to outsiders peeking in, her accommodations might have passed for a hippie dwelling.

No one in Tuscarora knew when or how the legend originated of three hundred hippie farmers living in caves and making their livelihood by cultivating three thousand acres of weed, but the numbers were constant as the tale resonated through the county and into neighboring states and back again. I overheard an embellishment one evening while I was sitting next to a helicopter pilot at a bar down the valley. He didn't recognize me; I had shaved and was wearing a cowboy hat. I remembered seeing him at a costume party in Tuscarora. I had been disguised as the Jolly Green Giant, wearing pea-green bathing trunks with my flesh dyed a matching shade from head to toes; Ben and Greg flanked me in miniature. Older townfolk attended the party dressed up impersonating their younger selves by wearing outfits quite fashionable three or four decades earlier. Half a dozen pottery students had arrived directly from the studio without washing up or changing into long pants. Their legs, ankles, and footwear were streaked with the distinctive yellow/orange of local clay and water.

On the evening of the costume party, the helicopter pilot had dropped in out of curiosity. That night his leather flight jacket and dark glasses passed easily as a costume. Later when I overheard him recollecting the event, he was answering a cowboy's question, "You been up there and seen them?"

"I saw only a few."

"So?"

"I can't say for sure how many are living in caves, but the ones I saw were certainly different." The pilot ordered another drink before continuing, "I know it's hard to believe, but I saw them . . . the oldest hippie had a big rat's nest of a beard and a shaved head. He came into the party holding hands with two little boys and . . . they were all of 'em painted green. Later some other hippies came in . . . looked like they were in their twenties and had never bathed. The girls wore no bras, and all of 'em wearing raggedly shorts and dirty T-shirts. Then I looked at their legs . . . it's hard to believe, but I-swear-to-God . . . these hippies had what looked to me like dried shit running down to their ankles."

Even though I was married with children, the original wife, two cars, etc., I was not naïve about the '60s drug culture. I knew of youth's desire to broaden the chemical horizon beyond the narrow, in-body limitations of estrogen or testosterone, and that maturing adults might be tempted to dabble with the out-of-body, mind-altering illegals that promised to lift humans to a higher, less sweaty plateau; but I also knew that in Nevada such activities carry the possibility of hard jail time.

New arrivals at the pottery school were briefed about Sheriff Harris, who from time to time would drop by unannounced to have a cup of coffee with me or watch the students throw pots. Long hair did not seem to bother him, but blatant criminal behavior might—a gentleman with a soft voice, an elegant tortoise-shell cigarette holder and no visible handgun, a law enforcer who prided himself on the few arrests made while he was in office. Still, I warned students that the man was certainly capable of being provoked. I asked that there be no lingering, second-hand dope-smoke in or around the hotel, so that if I were questioned I could honestly reply, "Not as far as I know."

Tuscarora students were probably as fascinated with recreational drugs as, say, students enrolled at Harvard or Boise State or the Sorbonne, but here in the mountains that behavior was inconspicuous.

Locals had visited the studios and chatted with the students, so they had a better grasp of artistic reality. Della always waved to new students from her garden and invited them over for a tour of the museum. Nona shouted at passing students, or Ben and Greg, to come over and help haul some firewood or move a heavy piece of furniture. Shouting was a form of endearment for Nona. She never shouted at a total stranger. Of course, Butters appreciated the potential to increase tavern business and the opportunity to retell his stories.

Acceptance of the family by valley ranchers came mostly through Ben and Greg's performance at school. On our first appearance at the grade school Christmas party, a rancher's wife approached Julie, introduced herself, and said, "I hear your boys are doing well. Not just that they are smart . . . my children tell me that Ben and Greg are just-good-kids!" After chatting a while longer, the wife closed by shaking hands and saying, "You know I've always believed that the fruit falls close to the tree." We had been validated by our produce.

When I was restless, in my late thirties, I tossed my hat into the countywide race for a seat on the school board. I reasoned not only that my education and experience would add depth to a board long dominated by ranchers and small businessmen but also that this position would help me gain acceptance in the wider community.

After filing papers at the courthouse in Elko, I returned home and kicked off the campaign by mail-ordering one thousand pencils with

Elect	MARK THE
DENNIS PARKS	← X
School Board	BALLOT

printed in red and blue on a white background with stars and stripes for a border. Prior to election day I rode in the Labor Day parade down the main street of Elko in the front seat of a metallic blue four-door Mercedes Benz on loan from a supporter. My boys and a visiting niece were at the open windows in back. While the car moved slowly, I waved to the crowds, and the kids giggled, aimed, and targeted the pencils. I couldn't blame them for trying to have fun on a hot afternoon. I couldn't criticize childishness either.

After the votes were tallied, I lost by a landslide to the incumbent but discovered that I was the favorite of Tuscarora and Independence Valley district voters by a margin of three votes. The incumbent, a long-time rancher in this valley, must have made enemies, but he had obviously campaigned more actively to the broader constituency while I stayed in my studio. This county is as large as five Belgiums, and I was not in a travel mood.

I conceded over the telephone and complimented the victor on his campaign. He in turn invited me to join the Independence Valley Fire Department, an invitation-only volunteer organization of which he was the chief. This honor was probably more appropriate for a young new-comer, certainly an honor worth far more that the cost of one thousand pencils.

■ Could concentric circles be the underlying pattern in human rela-tions: not a neat geometric pattern, but wiggly, wavy circles like those formed after a rock hits a pond? In the center were neighbors, the first to notice our intrusion and the first to become placid. Those circular waves that traveled to the perimeter took longer to calm. Julie and the boys were quickly accepted by the inner circle. Willis the rancher aided my acceptance with his caveat, "Remember he's a professor," i.e., harmless, eccentric. Had I been labeled an artist, the process would certainly have taken longer.

The two neighbors who contemplated shooting me dead are not ex-ceptions to the basic concentric rule because they came to Tuscarora af-ter we were settled. The gunmen were newcomers from a rough outer circle.

The concentric pattern can also be observed in my ceramic career, though ironically the wave action is reversed: recognition began on the periphery and flowed gradually inward. Ceramics have sold briskly to visitors from distant New York City, New Orleans, San Francisco, and Seattle, and regular buyers come from Las Vegas, Reno, and Elko. Invitations arrive by mail to exhibit around the country as well as to travel and work in exotic studios in Hungary, Poland, the Czech Republic, and Uzbekestan. Examples of my work have been acquired by museums in Italy, Belgium, England, and Russia. But with local shoppers in the Independence Valley I've had to wait longer for recognition. I probably don't need to understand this whole concentric phenomena.

▦ The strangers who drive the last seven miles into Tuscarora this summer will be on a road as rutted as it was when Julie, Ben, Greg, and I drove in almost forty years ago. There have been changes. Julie is now the postmaster after years of apprenticing as the part-time Saturday relief clerk. Hers is the first full-time paying job either of us has had in twenty-seven years. The post office was a squat, white, aluminum-sided, rectangular building. Julie contracted to have it painted a pale sage green. The American flag flying outside has often attracted tourists asking what they should see in Tuscarora. Julie knows where to send them. A tour of the studios will most likely be led by Ben, the new director/instructor at the pottery school.

After Ben graduated from Stanford in economics, he enrolled in English literature studies at the University of Nevada, Reno, and then finished off his education with a master of fine arts in ceramics at the Claremont Graduate University in California. He and his wife, Elaine, another M.F.A. in ceramics, are settled in the Fern Bush residence, our original home, where he was reared. After Mother's death, Julie and I moved down Main Street to the Plunkett house, where Mother had lived for fourteen years. From this house there is a better view of visitors coming and going at the hotel.

Every couple of months I pick Greg up at the Elko Airport when he arrives on a bargain, gambler-special flight from Santa Barbara. After he

Dennis and Ben Parks at the kiln. Ben is now a ceramic artist in his own right, and he also directs the Tuscarora Pottery School and manages the hotel. Photo by Julie Parks.

received his B.A. in biology at the University of California, Santa Cruz, he moved east for a doctorate in veterinary medicine at Ohio State. During his last semester he interned at an equine clinic in Southern California. He enjoyed the practice and stayed.

Both boys are still helpful during deer season. Urban exposure didn't rob them of their skills. Skinning and gutting an animal are as natural here as bicycling in suburbia: both difficult skills to acquire but undiminished by age.

Today the Independence Valley 4-H Club is still active, though we no longer know the children by name when they knock on the door at Christmastime to sing carols and receive our handout of candy canes. This was the first year they also came to our house on May Day and handed

Left to right: Ben, Dennis, and Greg Parks. Greg is an equine veterinarian practicing in Southern California. Photo by Julie Parks.

The Parks family in 1999. Left to right: Julie, Dennis, Ben, Elaine, and Greg. Photo by Ron Arthaud.

Dennis Parks at the potter's wheel. Photo by Larry Logan.

Julie a potted plant, a triple-blossom pink azalea, and a paper plate covered with homemade cream puffs. The little kids giggled when Julie thanked them.

After she set the gifts on our dining room table she lifted the Saran Wrap and sniffed, "These pastries smell wonderful, but don't you eat any . . . not with your intestines. Probably full of lactose." As she began nibbling, and before I walked to the kitchen to pour myself a glass of red, she commented, "D.P., you know life here has definitely changed. . . . It used to be that those 4-H kids only brought May Day flowers to the old people in town, like Nona, Della, Butters. . . . "